Eisen and Engler have written an outstan
who suffer from separation anxiety or schoc
the first of its type, describing practical, ste
that have been studied extensively in anxiety research
In addition to being a valuable resource for parents, this book will be very useful to teachers and mental health practitioners who work with anxious children.

—Martin M. Antony, Ph.D., ABPP, director of the Anxiety Treatment and Research Centre at St. Joseph's Healthcare and professor in the Departments of Psychiatry and Behavioural Neurosciences at McMaster University, both in Hamilton, ON

Separation anxiety can derail a child's normal development at any age. Moreover, it can make life miserable for that child's parents and family—not only the child. This book helps parents navigate the murky waters of separation anxiety by giving them a roadmap and a set of proven and effective strategies to help them deal with it and, yes, even to prevent it. In the hands of caring and motivated parents, it is a veritable tour de force. It is a well written, engaging, and eminently practical book. Parents (and their separation anxious children) will be thanking Eisen and Engler for years to come for their sage and helpful advice.

—Thomas H. Ollendick, Ph.D., university distinguished professor and director of the Child Study Center in the Department of Psychology at the Virginia Polytechnic Institute and State University in Blacksburg, VA

Eisen and Engler provide straightforward advice for parents of a child who is afraid of separation or afraid of school. Separation anxiety is a typical step in development for most children, but when it is interfering and present in older youngsters, then it merits attention. This step-by-step approach for parents, potentially used in conjunction with a therapist, offers sound advice and guidance that is consistent with the research evidence. The book is well-informed, organized, readable, and rich with examples.

—Philip C. Kendall, Ph.D., ABPP, Laura H. Carnell Professor of Psychology and Director of the Child and Adolescent Anxiety Disorders Clinic at Temple University in Philadelphia, PA

A highly user-friendly guide to help parents understand how to help children cope more effectively with separation anxiety and school refusal. Eisen and Engler are true leaders in the field of child anxiety. Their use of real life case illustrations really brings these evidence based skills home to parents and children. I would highly recommend this book to our own patients, to parents, to clinicians or graduate students working with children and families, and to all others who want to understand specific ways to help children with anxiety issues in ways that promotes their positive development.

—Donna B. Pincus, Ph.D., research associate professor and director of the Child and Adolescent Fear and Anxiety Treatment Program in the Center for Anxiety and Related Disorders at Boston University

Eisen and Engler have provided a wealth of information for parents about the do's and don'ts of helping their child with separation anxiety or school refusal. Clear, easy language, practical exercises, and real life examples are all based on the authors' hands-on experience and scientifically proven methods. This book is an essential resource for parents who are stuck in the binds produced by a separation anxious child and for therapists who are trying to provide an empirically validated program.

—Ronald M. Rapee, Ph.D., director of the Macquarie University Anxiety Research Unit and author of *Helping Your Anxious Child*

Eisen and Engler have written a clear, detailed guide for parents who are striving to support each child's autonomy and confidence. Supported by research and clinical insight, this book offers specific strategies to help children achieve healthy separation, while respectfully acknowledging the emotional lives of children and the need for parents to take care of themselves. Parenting is the most humbling effort, and this book supports this most important relationship in a child's life.

—Gerard Costa, Ph.D., director of the YCS Institute for Infant and Preschool Mental Health in East Orange, NJ

Helping Your Child Overcome Separation Anxiety *or* School Refusal

A STEP-BY-STEP GUIDE *for* PARENTS

ANDREW R. EISEN, PH.D.
LINDA B. ENGLER, PH.D.

New Harbinger Publications, Inc.

Publisher's Note

This publication is designed to provide accurate and authoritative information in regard to the subject matter covered. It is sold with the understanding that the publisher is not engaged in rendering psychological, financial, legal, or other professional services. If expert assistance or counseling is needed, the services of a competent professional should be sought.

Distributed in Canada by Raincoast Books.

New Harbinger Publications, Inc.
5674 Shattuck Avenue
Oakland, CA 94609

Cover design by Amy Shoup; Cover image by Brand X Pictures/PictureQuest (models only, used for illustrative purposes); Acquired by Catharine Sutker; Edited by Carole Honeychurch; Text design by Tracy Marie Carlson

Printed in the United States of America

Library of Congress Cataloging-in-Publication Data

Eisen, Andrew R.

Helping your child overcome separation anxiety or school refusal : a step-by-step guide for parents / Andrew R. Eisen and Linda B. Engler.

p. cm.

ISBN-13: 978-1-57224-431-3

ISBN-10: 1-57224-431-3

1. Separation anxiety in children. 2. School phobia. 3. Child rearing. I. Engler, Linda B. II. Title.

BF724.3.S38E36 2006

649'.154—dc22

2006010774

New Harbinger Publications' Web site address: www.newharbinger.com

08 07 06

10 9 8 7 6 5 4 3 2 1

First printing

To Cal and Phyllis Engler
for your unceasing love and support

To Mitchell Engler
for your wisdom, guidance, and friendship

To the parents and children we've worked with
for your courage, strength, and persistence

Contents

Foreword

Fear has always been a universal response to danger, designed to mobilize us to protect ourselves. No doubt, children's fears of separation arise initially from their need to ensure proximity to their parents for survival's sake. As aware of their dependent vulnerability as they are wishfully grandiose, though, they often develop irrational and unjustified fears. Whether perceived through the magical associations of a preschooler or the inflated invincibility of the adolescent, real dangers are easily confused with nonexistent ones. These may intensify transiently in the face of an external stress or as a predictable touchpoint of development unfolds. Occasionally, though, the fear of separation—like other fears—can become more entrenched, taking on a life of its own and taking with it the freedom of both children and their parents as it shackles them together.

Parents of separation-anxious children are bound to recognize themselves in *Helping Your Child Overcome Separation Anxiety and School Refusal*'s real-life stories, in the fears (of being left alone or abandoned, of getting sick, of a parent being harmed, or a catastrophic event), and in the different types of separation-anxious behavior that result. Parents may also recognize themselves in the carefully observed descriptions of the roles that children's fears can push parents to play, including "medical monitor," "security guard," "lifeguard," or "bodyguard." They'll come to better understand what has happened to their interactions with their children as a result and how they may even be inadvertently reinforcing their children's avoidant behavior.

Helping Your Child Overcome Separation Anxiety and School Refusal was written to aid parents in helping children discover their strengths as they face their fears of separation then take control of and master them. But this book also offers the support that parents will need as they realize that they must turn over some control and responsibility to their children, including the responsibility for experiencing and learning to tolerate anxiety. To do so, parents are gently guided by Drs. Eisen and Engler to consider the obstacles within that they may need to surmount in order to empower their children with greater self-reliance. The authors approach parents' feelings about letting go with understanding and respect and guide them through the concrete steps that they can help their children with.

This book carefully details instructions for a range of strategies, derived from widely accepted cognitive behavioral therapy principles, and adapts these for children of different ages and with different concerns. Special attention is devoted to school refusal, with careful differentiation of its brief and its more entrenched forms, including concrete advice for each. The authors rightly urge a prompt and organized response to the child who insists on staying home, since this behavior becomes so much harder to change with each added avoidant day.

Eisen and Engler's compassion for families bogged down by unwarranted fears shines through in the reassuring tone with which anxiety-provoking unknowns are addressed. Clear, practical information about what to expect as their recommendations are implemented and whether it is time to seek more help than any book can offer should make most families feel confident that they can be back in control.

A straightforward and hopeful book about how parents can help their children with a fairly common problem, *Helping Your Child Overcome Separation Anxiety and School Refusal* couldn't have been written at a more opportune time. How much harder it is today, for a child or for any of us, to know when we are safe and when to fear. Global warming, which might still be averted, is rendering our planet less hospitable, besieging us with an unpredictable succession of natural disasters—hurricanes, floods, and tidal waves—beyond our control. Acts of intolerance and hatred, which might still be overcome, lead to a vicious cycle of fear and more hatred, more terrorism and war. Too many communities have been fragmented by misunderstanding of differences and economic pressures into collections of isolated individuals who can no longer dare to care, though they might be emboldened to. Have we ever been at greater risk of being undone by our ever-mounting fears and our inability to distinguish the irrational ones from those that we must heed? Now, more than ever, children need our help in understanding their fears, where they come from, what they can do about them, and who can help them. They need help in sorting out the realistic fears from the irrational ones, the ones that they can do something about from the ones that they need our help with.

With simple, effective cognitive behavioral techniques so clearly set forth by Drs. Eisen and Engler, children learn that they are strong enough to handle their fears and to let go of their parents when they must. They will also begin to feel a sense of their own personal power and a greater sense of freedom. With the unbearable dependence of unrealistic fears of separation comes resentment. Yet when parents succeed in helping their children overcome separation anxiety, they will all feel freer and more open to love.

—Joshua Sparrow, MD

Acknowledgments

As always, our heartfelt thanks to Cal and Phyllis Engler for being the charter members of our fan club. To our children, Zachary and Carly, for making everything we do worthwhile. Special thanks to Catharine Sutker of New Harbinger Publications for encouraging us to write this book and for her enthusiasm, support, and guidance every step of the way. We also thank Carole Honeychurch, our editor, for her attention to detail and for helping us express our vision.

Introduction

I'm afraid to fall asleep at night. I know if I do, I'll find Lenore in our bed in the morning. She worries that every noise is an intruder breaking into the house. I don't know how to convince her that our house is safe. I'm exhausted!

Everyone tells me how well adjusted Debbie is. So why does she follow me around the house? I can't even go to the bathroom by myself. We have a great playroom downstairs, but Debbie still insists on watching TV in the kitchen while I prepare dinner. And if I put my foot down, she won't stop crying.

Lately, Peter wakes up every morning complaining that he is physically sick. He refuses to eat any of his breakfast. I can't take the stress of the morning routine anymore. It's affecting our whole family.

I feel like a doctor. The only difference is that I'm on call all the time. Mark won't go anywhere unless I promise to stay home or stay with him the entire time. I cannot remember the last time my husband and I socialized with friends.

—Parents of separation-anxious youth

THE WORLD OF THE SEPARATION-ANXIOUS CHILD

Do any of these scenarios sound familiar? These quotes help illustrate the world of separation-anxious children and their parents. If they sound a lot like what's going on in your family, don't despair—you're not alone. Separation anxiety is one of the most common problems in children, but it's also quite prevalent in adolescents and adults. How could this kind of problem be so common?

Sometimes it's difficult to understand why children who have never really experienced anything bad happening to them would worry about parental car accidents, household burglaries, or getting picked up late. It's easier to understand something like the development of a dog phobia when a child gets scratched by a dog.

Surprisingly, the majority of separation-related fears emerge without a specific triggering event. Keep in mind that nothing bad has to actually happen to a child and/or her family to set off separation anxiety. Even a community-wide or media-based catastrophe can easily set the stage for the development of separation anxiety.

On the other hand, you may have noticed that your child has always been sensitive and clingy and figured that her separation anxiety is a natural progression of these fears. Regardless of the source of separation anxiety, these fears can cause remarkable distress in children's lives. Many fears are largely temporary and part of normal development. This book, however, is about separation-related fears that may cause significant disruption in a child or adolescent's school functioning, friendships, and/or family life. In chapters 1 and 2, we'll discuss the specific types and possible causes of your child's separation anxiety and how they can be addressed in our program.

WHY YOU BOUGHT THIS BOOK

You likely purchased this book for any of the following reasons:

- You are sensitive to your child's signals and want to intervene early.
- You recognize that your child's struggles are not just a phase or simply due to immaturity.
- You're eager to learn as much as possible about separation anxiety so that you can help your child cope more effectively.
- You and/or your family are understandably overwhelmed by the stress caused by your child's separation anxiety.
- You realize that your child's current treatment is not working and/or desire a more skills-based, practical approach.
- This book was recommended by your child's therapist as a useful adjunct to help improve treatment success.

Regardless of your reasons, you did the right thing. Naturally, one of the goals of our book is to provide you with the tools to help your separation-anxious child cope more effectively. A second and perhaps more important goal, however, is to help you get your life back. After all, this book was written with you in mind.

GETTING YOUR LIFE BACK

As a loving parent, you may have sacrificed a great deal in your efforts to help your separation-anxious child. By doing so, you may have given up any or all of the following basic privileges:

- Sleep
- Hope for a peaceful morning routine
- Hobbies, exercise, or other recreational activities
- Social life
- Free time
- Freedom
- Privacy

We think it's about time that some sense of serenity is restored in your home. We believe that you are entitled to these basic privileges and shouldn't have to give them up to help your child. By committing to this book, you have taken the first step. Now it's our turn to show you how improving your life and helping your fearful child can happen at the same time. But first, a few words about our philosophy.

OUR PHILOSOPHY

Think of one of your proudest accomplishments. Did you achieve your goal overnight? Or did you at times become so overwhelmed with frustration and anxiety that you considered giving up altogether?

We all find ourselves in such a place at one time or another. Achieving the goal at hand seems impossible. At this point, you may feel that way about your child or adolescent's separation anxiety. You may have difficulty visualizing ever experiencing a sense of calm in your home again. Sleep deprivation can do that to you. Spending every waking moment with your child doesn't help either.

Your journey to more freedom is about to begin. Through a program that is clinically proven and based on the latest treatment research, we're going to show you how to manage, if not eliminate, your child's avoidance of separation-related situations. Of course, you'll have to do your part. We have found that certain expectations often help improve treatment success. As a result, we expect the following from you:

- Take small steps.
- Make a consistent effort.
- Be open to our suggestions.

In addition, you should expect the following from yourself:

- Do the best that you can.
- Refrain from blame.
- Focus on what you're doing to help.

HOW THIS BOOK CAN HELP YOU

We are indebted to David H. Barlow, Aaron T. Beck, Philip C. Kendall, Thomas H. Ollendick, and Wendy K. Silverman for their pioneering clinical research efforts. Without their work, this book would not have been possible.

Helping Your Child Overcome Separation Anxiety and School Refusal is intended to be used in several ways. For example, the book may be utilized as a step-by-step guide for parents who have not yet sought professional help. Reading this book can help educate you about the nature, development, and treatment of separation anxiety in children and adolescents. The book can also help you decide whether or not professional help is warranted.

Helping Your Child Overcome Separation Anxiety and School Refusal is designed to help parents with children experiencing mild to moderate separation anxiety and/or school refusal with minimal other problems. For best results, we encourage you to utilize the book in addition to working with a qualified therapist. In chapter 10, we discuss the benefits of working with a therapist, and in the resources section at the end of the book we provide a list of organizations and university-based child anxiety clinics that can serve as referral sources.

You can also use the book as a valuable resource for other family members and relatives who would like to better understand separation anxiety, school refusal, and related problems. Given that separation anxiety is often about having access to safe people, it's especially important that everyone involved in your child's care be on the same wavelength.

Finally, mental health professionals can offer *Helping Your Child Overcome Separation Anxiety and School Refusal* to anxious youth and their families as a collaborative companion to their treatment programs. For professionals seeking more comprehensive guidelines on how to treat separation anxiety and school refusal, we also recommend *Separation Anxiety in Children and Adolescents: An Individualized Approach to Assessment and Treatment* (Eisen and Schaefer 2005).

MAKING THE INVESTMENT

We're asking you to make an investment, one that we think is worthwhile. Separation anxiety is often associated with other problems such as worry, panic attacks, school refusal, and behavioral disorders. Early intervention may not only minimize/ eliminate your child's separation anxiety but could also prevent the development of later problems. The time to intervene is now. If you're ready and willing, we'll guide you every step of the way.

In the next ten chapters, we'll help you understand the different types of separation anxiety experienced in childhood and adolescence. In chapter 2, we begin to introduce four of the eight real-life stories that we will use to illustrate important concepts and treatment tools. In chapter 8, we complete our presentations by introducing the remaining four real-life stories (school refusal). All of these stories are drawn from our extensive clinical experience and represent composite sketches of typical families that we see in our practices. Of course, any distinguishing information has been disguised to protect the true identities of the families.

We'll demonstrate how to teach your child or adolescent relaxation techniques, cognitive therapy techniques, and problem-solving exercises. More importantly, we'll show you how to apply these coping tools to minimize your child's separation and/or school-related avoidance. Each chapter contains learning objectives to ensure the effective implementation of our program.

Are you ready? Let's get started. But first, we have to figure out the specific nature of your child's separation anxiety.

Chapter 1

Why Is Your Child Separation Anxious?

I feel sick. I can't eat breakfast.

—Peter

I heard a noise. What if someone breaks into the house?

—Lenore

CHAPTER OBJECTIVES

In this chapter you will learn:

- How to recognize the key features of your child's separation anxiety
- Some of the reasons for your child's fears
- Some of the causes of your child's separation anxiety

THE UNIVERSAL NATURE OF SEPARATION FEARS

Do you remember your childhood fears? Were you afraid of the dark? Were you afraid of dogs or spiders? Fears are a normal part of development and occur across cultures. They remain from our evolutionary past and help to keep us safe from potential danger.

Childhood fears are typically short lived. For example, a fear of strangers and separation distress often emerges within the first year of life and usually fades by the second or third year.

However, some children continue to experience crying, clinging, and sadness upon separating from primary caregivers. Other children may first develop separation anxiety at three or four years of age. Specific fears (like being afraid of the dark or of supernatural figures), unpleasant bodily feelings (like stomachaches, nausea), or general worries about catastrophic events (for instance, burglaries, kidnappings) are often the culprits.

During the elementary-school years, separation anxiety may evolve into full-fledged separation anxiety disorder, with fears of being alone and/or being abandoned (Eisen and Schaefer 2005). A child's greater understanding of the world around him coupled with exposure (real or imagined) to actual environmental dangers (for example, natural disasters) increases the likelihood that the child will perceive potential catastrophes as inevitable.

In addition, as children get older, fears may become more performance based (around test taking or athletic competition) and/or socially oriented (self-consciousness). However, if separation-related fears remain unaddressed, adjustment problems may continue well into young adulthood.

WHAT DOES SEPARATION ANXIETY LOOK LIKE?

Every child experiences separation anxiety in his own unique way. Most children, however, share some common features, including a fear of being alone and/or a fear of being abandoned.

Don't Leave Me Alone

You may have noticed that your child often avoids being alone somewhere in the house, especially when other family members are present elsewhere. There may be particular areas of the house that are more difficult for your child to stay alone in than others, like a bedroom or bathroom. Your child may only feel safe when he can:

- Hear a family member in a nearby room
- See a family member in a nearby room
- Be with a family member (within touching distance) at all times

The first two situations are likely to be less disruptive to the natural routines of family life than the third. Some children may be able to stay alone as long as an activity, like schoolwork or video games, keeps their thoughts occupied. But most children will still be on the alert for signs that a family member is moving away from them in the house. For example, they may call out

"Where are you going?" or make excuses to follow you (for instance, helping you with what you're doing). On the other hand, when a child needs to move to another space in the house, he will let a family member know or may encourage younger siblings to tag along.

It's not surprising that being alone at night tends to be more difficult than during the day. Darkness makes even the simplest tasks more ominous (taking a bath, or brushing one's teeth alone). One of the most common problems that children and adolescents report is a fear of sleeping alone. If your child is afraid to sleep alone, you may be experiencing occasional or frequent:

- Visits to your bedroom
- Sleepovers in your bed or on the floor
- Sleepovers in your child's bed, trundle/bunk bed, chair, or floor

You may be exhausted from constant power struggles or lack of sleep if you have attempted to take your child back to his bedroom. On the other hand, for the sake of your family's sanity, you may have surrendered to spending the night with your child. In any event, following through with our program will help to restore much-needed freedom, privacy, and sleep.

Don't Leave Me Here

You may have noticed that your child may resist or refuse to attend school, playdates, extracurricular activities, social events, or sleepovers unless you promise to remain nearby. If your child fears being abandoned, he may be fine during the event, especially if you stay close by. But getting him there may be an exhausting endeavor. Abandonment fears often occur when children are apprehensive about being expected to stay without a parent and/or about the possibility of the parent not picking them up. Separation-anxious apprehension may vary according to:

- Duration (a few minutes to several hours)
- Intensity (mild tantrums to full-blown panic)

It's perfectly understandable if you've decided to pick your battles and only demand your child's attendance for obligatory situations (like school or religious studies). Forcing your child to attend extracurricular activities may not seem worth it, given the undue stress for everyone involved. School refusal is likely to be a problem as well, unless of course you've become a prisoner of your home or constantly on call. Rest assured, if you follow through with our program, your child will learn to feel more secure and you will get your life back. Let's examine some of the reasons for your child's separation anxiety.

REASONS FOR YOUR CHILD'S SEPARATION ANXIETY

By now you recognize that your child fears being alone and/or being abandoned. At the same time, however, you may wonder why this is the case, especially if no logical reason exists for the fearful behavior. In our experience, separation anxiety is often kept going by a fear of getting sick and/or worry about catastrophic events.

Feeling Sick

Are you sensitive to the physical feelings in your body? Do you often suspect that you are becoming ill long before your physician confirms this to be the case? Is your stomach easily upset from unfamiliar foods? If so, you are also in a position to accurately make a connection between the source of your physical discomfort and its logical cause. But, what happens when a child feels this way?

Children often complain of unpleasant feelings (for instance, stomachaches, headaches, and dizziness) before having to separate from a trusted adult. But given their young age, they are less likely to make the connection between the upcoming separation and the physical feeling. In addition, children are more likely to link the physical discomfort to an unpleasant outcome (something like vomiting). Thus, the *fear* of getting sick keeps a child's separation anxiety going. It doesn't matter that your child rarely if ever actually gets sick. Rather, he gets caught up in a dynamic of fear being misinterpreted as potential illness, as illustrated below:

Anticipated separation

⇩

Bad physical feeling

⇩

Fear of getting sick

REAL OR IMAGINED?

Where are these physical feelings coming from? There may be an element of truth to your child's fear of getting sick. For example, he may have once suffered from a stomach virus and vomited. This incident may be recent or may have occurred many years ago. However, now any time your child has an unpleasant stomach sensation, he fears getting sick again.

On the other hand, there may not be any actual unpleasant physical events that you can think of. Rather, your child has always been sensitive to the physical feelings in his body. Simply observing another family member become sick or hearing about another child's illness can encourage the fear as well.

Feeling Worried

You may have noticed that your child with separation anxiety also worries about dangerous events happening to him or to someone else in the family (for instance, someone being robbed, kidnapped, or in a car accident). Just knowing that he will have to separate may trigger these worries in your child. Younger children may fear that something generally bad will occur, whereas older children and adolescents may dread the likelihood of specific personal catastrophes, as illustrated below:

Anticipated separation

⇩

Worry

⇩

Fear of catastrophic event

REAL OR IMAGINED?

You may wonder why your child is worried about family safety, especially if nothing bad has ever happened to you or your child. Remember, this is all about your child's perception. Did you ever pick your child up a few minutes late from school, a playdate, or party? Were you ever in even a small fender bender? Has your child ever heard you express your fears or worries about safety issues? These normally occurring events can easily become overgeneralized in an already anxious child who has difficulty interpreting the events accurately.

On the other hand, a catastrophe reported from television, the radio, or local newspaper may be the culprit. If you're lucky, you may be relatively successful in shielding your child from disturbing newsworthy events. What about movies, however, that he sees at school or a friend's house? Sometimes it may be difficult to distinguish fact from fiction, especially for younger children. Even older children and adolescents can easily become spooked from scary movies. Disastrous events, real or imagined, are never in short supply, and may be lurking just around the corner from the mind of your separation-anxious child.

ANXIETY CONTINUING PAST THE TYPICAL AGE

Thus far, we've discussed the form (fear of being alone and/or abandoned) and some reasons (fear of sickness and/or catastrophic worry) for your child's separation anxiety. What may be harder to grasp, however, is why your child's separation anxiety continues past the typical age of three to six years. The continuation of separation anxiety is best understood by the cycle of avoidance (Ollendick 1998).

The Cycle of Avoidance

Think of the last time you had a meal that didn't agree with you. We've all had such meals. Most likely our discomfort involved some serious indigestion. In addition, our experience may have been specific to a particular restaurant or dinner party. However, we may now be reluctant to sample similar foods in other situations or settings.

Why are we afraid to try again? Simply thinking about the food makes us uncomfortable. And the longer we wait, the more unpleasant the idea of eating the same food becomes, and the less likely we'll try again. Avoidance (of the food) ensures temporary relief, but ultimately keeps us afraid. The same is true regarding your child's anxiety.

Most children's separation anxiety is sustained by avoiding situations that are perceived as potentially dangerous to them or others. Evidence suggests that the likelihood of such situations occurring is very slim, but every time a child avoids a separation-related situation, he believes that disaster was prevented. Thus, avoidance only leads to more avoidance.

Yet, why are we sometimes reluctant to help separation-anxious children confront their fears? Like the food example, simply thinking about being separated may evoke a strong fear response in your child, usually in the form of symptoms and/or catastrophic worry. As loving parents, the last thing we want is to see our children experience discomfort.

It may seem surprising, but children will only be able to conquer separation anxiety if they *confront* and *feel* the fear. For example, your child needs to learn that nothing bad will happen to him or others if left alone or dropped off somewhere. Until that happens, your child will always assume the worst-case scenario. Thus, it will become your job to teach your child that nothing bad will happen to him.

In the next section, we address your most important question: What has caused my child to become separation anxious?

SOME CAUSES

What is the root of your child's separation anxiety? A simple question deserves a simple answer. We wish the answer could be traced to a single stressful event. That would make understanding separation anxiety so much easier. Yet, a large amount of research (see Eisen and Schaefer 2005), as well as our many years of clinical experience, suggests that separation anxiety is the result of many factors. Separation anxiety may be best understood by examining biological, environmental, and psychological sensitivities. First, let's examine the biological/genetic factor.

Your Child's Personality

Every child comes into this world with certain sensitivities to emotional experiences. Some children are naturally outgoing and confident whereas others are shy and fearful. We are referring to your child's temperament or personality. Research suggests that children prone to anxiety may be more emotionally sensitive than the average child (Lonigan et al. 2004). This means that your child is likely more fearful, cautious, or clingy. In addition, he may have difficulty adjusting to unfamiliar or unexpected separation-related situations.

Recognizing that your child is emotionally sensitive may be nothing new, and at times this factor may be easy to dwell on. But remember, there are no good or bad temperaments. Rather, each style is associated with advantages and disadvantages. On the positive side, having an emotionally sensitive child means you are the parent of a loving, sweet, and affectionate person. We would never want to change those qualities. Our goals are to help you capitalize on your child's strengths, take into account his sensitivities (rather than to take them personally), and to facilitate his independence and problem-solving abilities.

Your Family Tree

Anxiety tends to run in families. Chances are that you, your spouse, or a close relative also experiences some form of anxiety. At first glance, you may blame yourself or hold another family member responsible for your child's separation anxiety. What gets passed down, however, is a general biological sensitivity (Barlow 2002). It may get expressed as anxiety, panic, sadness, or better yet, not at all. It's no one's fault. It's part of our heritage, just like our looks, height, hair color, or athletic ability.

Do you still feel the burden? Is it because you currently experience anxiety or panic, or because you struggled with separation fears as a child? Even if this is true, your child's anxiety is still not your fault. If anything, you may have a greater appreciation of what it feels like to experience anxiety. Your sensitivity, undoubtedly, will be a powerful tool in helping to eliminate your child's fear of separation.

Your Family Environment

Biological sensitivity sets the stage for the development of separation anxiety, usually in the form of an increased sensitivity to physical feelings, worry, or difficulty adjusting to unfamiliar situations. The family environment, however, can unintentionally help sustain a child's separation anxiety.

Believe it or not, it's easy to encourage these feelings, and every parent does it, even with the best of intentions. Simply reassuring your child (for instance, "Don't worry, I'll pick you up early") during separation-related situations will actually keep your child's anxiety going. What parent wouldn't want to reassure their child that there's nothing to worry about? But in reality, reassurance is another form of avoidance.

In chapter 3, we'll help you understand how parenting styles impact separation anxiety. More importantly, we'll discuss parenting strategies that will help keep your child's separation-anxious avoidance to a minimum.

Stressful Life Events

Common stressful situations can increase your child's anxiety level, either directly or indirectly. For example, family-related stressors (like a grandparent's illness) may directly increase your child's fears about your well-being, make him more sensitive to the experience of separation-related stress, and ultimately result in increased avoidance of separation-related scenarios. On the other hand, peer issues or school problems may indirectly heighten the amount of separation anxiety your child experiences simply by increasing your child's overall stress level. For example, stress related to academic difficulties may decrease your child's ability to handle routine separations.

We believe that it's possible to break the cycle of avoidance. This is best accomplished by encouraging children to have positive experiences that can change the negative thoughts they have about a stressful event. For example, when children are unsuccessful in confronting feared situations, it is important to encourage them to try again (for example, at school, a sleepover, or camp), being sure that they have new tools to help prepare them for more successful experiences. But remember, success is simply a child's perception. Research shows that separation-anxious children often overestimate the potential threat in situations (Bogels and Zigterman 2000). As a result, we'll show you how to help your child evaluate separation-related events more realistically (to be discussed in chapter 5).

Your Child's Sense of Security

As you can see, there are many factors involved in the development and continuation of a child or adolescent's separation anxiety. Trying to uncover a single cause may prove to be an impossible task. And while this complexity may be disheartening, the good news is that we can minimize and/or eliminate your child's separation anxiety without knowing the exact causes. We cannot change your child's genetic background, nor can we alter his past. What we can help you change is your child's reaction to separation-related situations.

Presently, because of various sensitivities, your child may feel insecure and apprehensive when confronted with anticipated separations. He may cling to you for constant support. Throughout the book, we'll teach you how to help your child feel more secure so that he can successfully manage separation-related situations.

Please take a moment to complete our end-of-chapter learning check. Your answers will help you develop your child's separation-fears list(s) in chapter 4.

LEARNING CHECK: MY CHILD'S SEPARATION ANXIETY

Circle all that apply.

The key features of my child's separation anxiety include:

Being alone day night while sleeping

Being abandoned home school extracurricular social events

My child's separation anxiety is sustained by:

Fear of sickness home school extracurricular social events

Catastrophic worry him/her me spouse entire family

My child avoids:

Being alone occasionally sometimes most of the time

Being dropped off occasionally sometimes most of the time

Summary

In this chapter we helped you understand the key features, reasons, and possible causes of your child's separation anxiety. In chapter 2, we'll explain the relationship between these fears and his specific safety needs. In addition, we also introduce some real-life stories of separation-anxious youth and their families. Throughout the book we'll use these families as examples to show you how to effectively help your own child or adolescent.

Chapter 2

Understanding Your Child's Safety Needs

Lenore was waking us up every night. We couldn't go without sleep anymore. What choice did we have but to let her sleep with us?

—Kate

Peter has become such a homebody. He's not interested in going out with us or his friends. I'm starting to get concerned. It's not natural for a fourteen-year-old to be this way.

—Mary

CHAPTER OBJECTIVES

In this chapter you will learn:

- Why your child with separation anxiety seeks safety
- The relationship between your child's separation anxiety and her specific safety needs
- How to recognize the four types of separation anxiety

SEEKING SAFETY

Imagine that you need to give a speech in front of hundreds of people, or you need to visit someone in a far-off place that makes you feel uncomfortable. You might wear your lucky suit or pack a talisman to help you feel more secure. We call items like these *safety signals,* and they are things that help us to feel protected in ambiguous situations and include safe people, places, objects, or actions (Barlow 2002).

Safety Signals and Separation Anxiety

Separation anxiety is largely about being near safe people. Naturally, children will come to depend more on safe places (parent's room), objects (a water bottle), or actions (following a parent around the house) if, for some reason, they are less able to reach safe people. Safety signals in the form of transitional objects (like a stuffed animal) may be considered age appropriate. Sometimes, however, a child may appear to be coping with a separation, but it is only because the safety signal is present.

For example, if you spend the night with your child or remain at a birthday party for the entire time, she'll sleep through the night or have fun at the party. Only when you decide to step out might your child react with fear. Remember, children will only be able to conquer separation anxiety if they *confront* and *feel* the fear.

Children need to realize that even after separations, they are still safe. Safety signals serve as another form of avoidance. Thus, the idea will be to gradually remove your child's safety signals (see chapter 4) so she learns that, though she may feel anxious, she is still safe and secure.

SPECIFIC SAFETY NEEDS

In the upcoming sections, we discuss how different combinations of circumstances and fear reactions prompt specific safety needs in separation-anxious youth. We'll then refer to each relationship as a specific type of separation anxiety and illustrate each with a real-life story. First, let's examine the safety needs that emerge when a fear of being alone (during the day) is sustained by a fear of getting sick.

Being Alone, Fear of Sickness, and Personal Safety

A child's fear of getting sick during the day prompts the need for a medical monitor—some trusted person to stay nearby just in case sickness occurs. As you can see, a medical monitor removes a child's separation anxiety simply by being available.

Being alone

⇩

Fear of sickness

⇩

Need for a medical monitor

When a fear of being alone is sustained by a fear of becoming ill and not having someone available to help, we use the term "the follower" to capture this relationship. The child continually follows the parent around so the parent will always be available in the event that the child feels ill. We illustrate with our real-life story of Debbie and her mother, Janice.

THE FOLLOWER

In many ways, Debbie is a typical seven-year-old girl. She loves school, gymnastics, ice skating, and playing with her friends. On playdates, other mothers report that Debbie is well behaved, respectful, and a pleasure to have around. Her teacher describes her as sweet, kind, and an eager learner.

At home, however, Debbie follows her mother around the house. During the day she refuses to spend time in her room alone without the promise of Janice being nearby and checking on her every few minutes. Debbie does her homework in the kitchen while Janice prepares dinner. She tags along as Janice does the laundry, throws out the garbage, talks on the phone, and goes to the bathroom. Debbie refuses to play in the downstairs playroom, and if pressed, she holds her stomach, cries, or throws a temper tantrum. When Janice is not around, Debbie forces her four-year-old brother, Ray, to stay with her.

Being Alone, Worry, and Personal Safety

Older children and adolescents are typically more afraid than younger ones to be alone at night. This is simply because older kids have a better idea of bad things that *could* occur than small children. This fear is often sustained by worry about catastrophic events (for instance, an intruder), and as such, prompts the need for a "security guard."

Being alone

⇩

Fear of an intruder

⇩

Need for a security guard

In this scenario, children need someone to protect them from potential break-ins. Some children may not feel safe unless someone watches over them for the entire night. As a result, a child may repeatedly visit or demand to stay with her parents in the evening. When a fear of being alone continues under these circumstances, we use the term "the visitor" to capture this relationship. We illustrate with our real-life story of Lenore and her parents, Kate and Jack.

THE VISITOR

Kate and Jack describe their ten-year-old daughter, Lenore, as an excellent student, athletic, well liked by her peers, and very responsible at home. Her teachers describe her as a model child. Yet, Lenore is shy, sensitive, and nervous, and despite her accomplishments, she lacks self-confidence. Lenore has also been sleeping in her parents' bed for the last three months.

Lenore is terrified that an intruder will break into the house. Despite an absence of break-ins in her neighborhood or surrounding areas, Lenore panics at the slightest noise, such as the wind, the radiator banging, or a passing car. Lenore can spend time alone in different rooms of the house during the day (when someone is home). After dinner, however, she becomes apprehensive and requires reassurance that she will be spending the night in her parents' bedroom.

Being Abandoned, Fear of Sickness, and Personal Safety

When a fear of being abandoned is sustained by a fear of getting sick, the need for a "lifeguard" emerges.

Being dropped off

⇩

Fear of sickness

⇩

Need for a lifeguard

When children leave their home for activities, the possibility of getting sick has more serious implications. A child may panic at the thought of becoming ill outside of the home where a trusted person may not be available. As a result, children may refuse to go places without having access to someone who can rescue them, like a teacher, nurse, coach, or friend. If trusted persons are unavailable, children may engage in safety behaviors (carrying a water bottle, avoiding eating) to minimize their anxiety. When a fear of being abandoned is continued under these circumstances, we use the term "the misfortune teller" to capture this relationship. We illustrate with our real-life story of Peter and his parents, Rick and Mary.

THE MISFORTUNE TELLER

Fourteen-year-old Peter is an avid sports fan. He watches every game on television and keeps statistics in his head. He plays all sports and especially loves baseball and basketball. Unlike many adolescents, however, Peter's favorite activity is to stay at home. Other than socializing with his friends at school or while playing on the baseball team, Peter rarely sees them. He never goes over to friends' houses and rarely even attends outings with his family.

Peter's parents, Rick and Mary, explain that their son has always been sensitive to the physical feelings in his body. Each morning he says that he feels sick and is convinced that he will throw up. As a result, he skips both breakfast and lunch and repeatedly visits the nurse and/or goes to the bathroom at school. Peter also carries a water bottle so he will have something to drink readily available in case he becomes nauseous. After school, Peter hangs around his baseball coach until his mother picks him up.

Being Abandoned, Worry, and Parental Safety

When a fear of being abandoned is sustained by worry about parental safety, the child's need to act as a parental "bodyguard" emerges.

Being abandoned

⇩

Worry about parental safety

⇩

Parental bodyguard

In this scenario, children constantly monitor a parent's specific whereabouts throughout the day, since they fear for their parent's safety. Children may only separate if the parent promises to stay home or pick them up early. Any sign of lateness on the parent's part means disaster has struck. Children often need constant reassurances about where and when a parent will be available. Some children may not separate unless they have immediate access to the parent (in person, by phone, cell phone, or beeper).

When a fear of being abandoned is sustained under these circumstances, we use the term "the timekeeper" to capture the relationship. We illustrate with our real-life story of Mark and his mother, Peggy.

THE TIMEKEEPER

Mark is a sensitive nine-year-old boy. He loves karate and video games and enjoys spending time with his family. But Mark has few friends and will only consider having playdates at his house. Mark refuses to attend birthday parties, karate class (unless his mother stays for the entire class), school field trips, and sleepovers. Mark also refuses to take the school bus. Each morning before Peggy drops him off at school, Mark insists that she promise to stay home so that he won't have to worry about her.

When Peggy goes shopping, Mark calls his mother repeatedly on her cell phone until she returns home. Peggy is tired and frustrated and believes Mark should be over this worry by now.

To help you keep track of the relationship between the different types of separation anxiety and specific safety needs, please refer to the following table.

Separation Anxiety Types and Safety Needs

Separation Anxiety Type	Safety Needs	Real-Life Story
Follower Fear of being alone (day), sustained by a fear of getting sick	*Medical Monitor* Someone to stay nearby just in case sickness occurs	*Debbie (7)* Parent: Janice Brother: Ray (4)
Visitor Fear of being alone (night), sustained by a fear of an intruder	*Security Guard* Someone to remain alert at night for signs of a break-in	*Lenore (10)* Parents: Kate and Jack
Misfortune Teller Fear of being abandoned, sustained by a fear of getting sick	*Lifeguard* Someone to remain nearby who can prevent/protect from serious illness	*Peter (14)* Parents: Rick and Mary
Timekeeper Fear of being abandoned, sustained by worry about parental safety	*Parental Bodyguard* Child needs constant access to parent's whereabouts by sight, sound, or parental promises to stay home	*Mark (9)* Parent: Peggy

Please take a moment to complete our end-of-chapter learning check. Your answers will help you complete your child's safety-needs list(s) in chapter 4.

LEARNING CHECK: MY CHILD'S SAFETY NEEDS

Circle all that apply

My child's safety needs most closely resemble the:

Medical monitor   Security guard   Lifeguard   Parental bodyguard

My child's safe persons include:

Self/spouse   Relative   Teacher   Nurse   Coach   Friend

My child's safe places include:

Home   Parent/sibling room   Relative's house   Friend's house

My child's safe objects include:

Night-light   Blankie/stuffed animal   Toy/book   Food/drink

My child's safe actions include:

Shadowing   Sleeping with others   Phone calls   Promises

Summary

In this chapter, we discussed the relationship between your child's type of separation anxiety (follower, visitor, misfortune teller, and timekeeper) and her specific safety needs. We also explained how to determine the extent that your child's separation anxiety is interfering with family life. In chapter 3, we help you understand your child's behavior and its relationship to different parenting styles.

Chapter 3

Understanding Your Child's Behavior

Every day is the same. Debbie follows me everywhere I go. If I want to go to the bathroom by myself, she throws a tantrum. She's seven years old now! She really knows how to push my buttons.

—Janice

CHAPTER OBJECTIVES

In this chapter you will learn:

- How to recognize the four parenting styles that accompany separation anxiety
- How to view your child's separation anxiety in a healthy way
- How to minimize power struggles and encourage your child's coping through shaping and modeling

YOUR PARENTING STYLE

To help you fully understand your child's behavior, we'll present our four key parenting styles that are common in families of separation-anxious children. The features of these parenting styles are based on current research (Rapee 1997). We illustrate some of the reasons for each style and discuss their implications for separation-anxiety management using each of our real-life family stories.

The Peacekeeper

The peacekeeper neither encourages nor discourages his child with separation anxiety from confronting his fears. The peacekeeper's neutral position may arise from a parent's own low-key personality or in response to his child's temperament. For example, a child who is more intense (strong willed and oppositional) may increase a parent's desire to keep the peace. On the other hand, when a child is more passive, the peacekeeping parent may not realize that more effort is needed to address his child's fears.

Peter's parents, Rick and Mary, fit the peacekeeper parenting style. For example, they both possess low-key dispositions. As such, they don't view Peter's morning nausea as a big deal, especially since he goes to school without a fuss. Peter's passive nature also limits him from revealing his fears or his dependence on safe persons and objects outside his home. Since he appears to be doing well with academics, baseball, and social relationships, Rick and Mary are not overly concerned.

THE BOTTOM LINE

If you're a peacekeeper, your child may not be experiencing regular separation-related confrontations. As a result, his separation anxiety will likely get stronger over time through avoidance of fearful situations. We'll help you make more active efforts to help him confront his fears.

The Negotiator

The negotiator makes some active efforts to help his child with separation anxiety confront his fears. In the end, however, the negotiator may back off and give in to the child's anxiety. This pulling back is usually in response to a child's temperament. For example, strong-willed and oppositional children may strongly resist any parental efforts to expose them to separation-related scenarios. As a result, it may seem easier to just end the negotiation and let the child avoid.

On the other hand, if a child is more passive, he is likely to obediently comply with exposures. However, the child may develop a greater dependence on safety signals to help him through. Thus, even though the child seems to be confronting anxiety-provoking situations, he is not actively facing his fear. Either way, a good amount of avoidance will still be occurring.

Debbie's mother, Janice, fits the negotiator parenting style. She isn't happy with Debbie's tag-along behaviors and resents the loss of her freedom and privacy. She encourages Debbie to spend some time alone in her room and the downstairs playroom and lets Debbie know that she needs privacy when she goes to the bathroom. When Debbie won't budge, Janice insists that she try to do these things. But Debbie always responds with "I can't," holds her stomach, and throws a temper tantrum. To prevent a prolonged outburst, Janice tends to give in to Debbie's demands.

THE BOTTOM LINE

If you're a negotiator, you're on the right track. You recognize that your child's separation anxiety is interfering with family life, and you are willing to help him confront his fears. When your child's resistance is strong, however, you may not be sure how to carry on. We'll help you pick your battles so you can know when to stand firm with your limit setting while still preserving your sanity.

The Protector

The protector makes some active efforts to help his child with separation anxiety avoid fears. The protector's cautious stance may reflect a parent's desire to keep his child safe, in this case by shielding him from potential anxiety-provoking scenarios. While such a parenting style can be admirable and often carried out with loving intentions, a parent may go too far and overprotect his child.

Sometimes, however, the protector parenting style stems from a parent's own anxiety. For example, worrying about or observing a child who is experiencing distress may be too upsetting. As a result, a parent may limit activities (like sleepovers) or choose not to discuss circumstances (for instance, a funeral) that may trigger anxiety in his child. Ordinarily, such a protective stance is perfectly natural as long as situations are deemed too disturbing, given the child's age. Parental overprotection only becomes problematic when it significantly hinders a child's age-appropriate activities and emotional growth.

Kate, Lenore's mother, fits the protector parenting style. She can see Lenore's demeanor change soon after dinner. It breaks her heart to watch Lenore get anxious simply thinking about sleeping in her room alone, and it's easier for Kate to reassure Lenore that she can spend the night in Kate's bed if she needs to. Kate's difficulty setting limits with Lenore isn't restricted to her daughter's separation anxiety. Kate also has a hard time saying no in general. She wants to ask her husband, Jack, for help with Lenore but is afraid to have an argument with him. As a result, she lies in bed each night watching her husband and daughter sleep peacefully.

THE BOTTOM LINE

If you're a protector, your child may not be experiencing severe enough separation anxiety to be causing family conflict. This is because you are likely giving in to his fearful demands. You may realize that this lenience isn't such a good thing anymore, but you're not sure how to change things, especially if you don't have a lot of support. We'll show you how to gradually challenge your child, allow him to experience some anxiety, and still help him feel secure.

The Evaluator

The protector may go too far in discouraging his child to confront separation-related fears. The evaluator, on the other hand, may go too far in encouraging these confrontations. The evaluator's strong stance may stem from his unrealistic expectations regarding a child's ability to handle separation anxiety. As a result, the evaluator is often disappointed with the child's progress and may evaluate outcomes in an overly critical way. Such critical overtones may also be the product of a tired parent who is frustrated with regular intrusions and disruptions to his family life.

Peggy fits the evaluator parenting profile. She believes that her son, Mark, is too old to still be experiencing separation anxiety. She has difficulty accepting the limitations that go along with Mark's fears. As a result, even small successes are easily dismissed. Peggy is also tired and frustrated from dealing with the constant interruptions imposed on her lifestyle. She is growing to resent Mark and is having difficulty understanding her son's resistance to confronting separation-related situations.

THE BOTTOM LINE

If you're an evaluator, you're on the right track in the sense that your child does need to confront separation-related situations. But it's important to understand that children have to confront their fears at their own pace. If you push too hard, your child may shut down and refuse to make any effort at all. Also, separation anxiety can occur at any age. Even though Mark is nine, he is much younger emotionally. Thus, Peggy needs to adjust her expectations to reflect Mark's emotional needs. We'll help you set up a realistic and appropriate set of exposures so that your child can make good progress while still feeling relatively secure. We'll also help you to appreciate the value of small successes.

To help you keep track of the relationship between the different parenting styles and separation anxiety, please refer to the following table.

Parenting Styles and Separation Anxiety		
Parenting Style	**Objective**	**Real-Life Story**
Peacekeeper Neither encourages nor discourages separation-related exposures	*Activate Efforts* Implement regular exposures	*Rick and Mary* Child: Peter (Misfortune teller)
Negotiator Encourages separation-related exposures but may back off in the face of resistance	*Continue Efforts* Choose your battles, work on limit setting	*Janice* Child: Debbie (Follower)
Protector Discourages separation-related exposures	*Activate Efforts* Gradually implement regular exposures	*Kate and Jack* Child: Lenore (Visitor)
Evaluator Encourages separation-related exposures but in an overly forceful or critical way	*Continue Efforts* Emphasize your child's small successes, work on realistic goal setting	*Peggy* Child: Mark (Timekeeper)

VIEWING YOUR CHILD'S ANXIETY

At this point, you have a better understanding of the specific nature of your child's separation anxiety and some general parenting styles that may accompany it. But how do you see your child's separation anxiety? Let's discuss the bad, the ugly, the good, and the healthy.

The Bad

Is your child manipulative? Janice certainly felt that way. Why did Debbie have to follow her around the house all the time? After all, she seemed okay to be alone in her room as long as she was watching television. So, since Debbie could sometimes stay alone in her room, Janice felt her behavior had to be manipulative.

On one hand, Janice is right. Debbie *could* stay alone in her room. Does this mean that Janice should expect her to stay alone all the time? Not necessarily. We need to look at Debbie's anxiety and the safety signals present in each separation-related situation.

For example, let's take a closer look at Debbie's behavior to see under what circumstances she can feel okay to be alone in her room. It seems Debbie is more willing to stay when Janice agrees to be her medical monitor (check on her every few minutes). When Janice is preoccupied with family responsibilities and cannot check on her, Debbie either follows her mom or gets her younger brother, Ray, to hang out with her. Thus, when Janice is unavailable and Debbie is not preoccupied, should Janice be surprised that Debbie keeps seeking her attention? Not really. If she is surprised, however, Janice is likely to view Debbie's behavior as manipulative. Thinking of your child's behavior this way will likely foster more negative interactions and greater feelings of resentment.

What may look like manipulation, however, are often a child's desperate attempts to avoid feeling anxious. The attention-getting behavior (like whining, crying, or throwing tantrums) shows you that he is overwhelmed and cannot cope. We prefer to view these attention-getting behaviors as survival tactics rather than acts of willful disobedience.

The Ugly

When we assume that a child's behavior is manipulative, we are more likely to take his actions personally and as signs of disrespect. In these cases, it's only natural that we attempt to reestablish authority. The ugliness of the resulting power struggles largely depends on the interplay among a child's temperament, safety needs, and a parent's response style.

For example, let's take a look at the dynamic brewing between Mark (timekeeper) and his mother Peggy (evaluator). First, Mark is strong willed. This means that if he believes that he cannot cope, he may fiercely resist separation-related confrontations. Mark also possesses a high intensity temperament. As a result, he is likely to experience strong reactions (positive and negative) to situations. Finally, Mark has unrelenting safety needs (parental bodyguard). This means that he will do everything in his power to make sure that his mother is safe during separations.

How will Peggy's parenting style mesh with her son's? As you can imagine, there is great potential for intense power struggles. Peggy is likely to view Mark's refusal to attend extracurricular activities as oppositional behavior (rather than fear). In addition, she resents (rather than accepts as part of genuine anxiety) Mark's constant intrusions. As a result, Peggy may respond in an overly critical and forceful way. Escalating power struggles are likely to ensue as mother and son fight to maintain control.

Each of our real-life family stories presents its own unique challenges (to be discussed in chapters 4, 6, and 7). Sometimes when we get caught up in power struggles (winning by establishing authority or losing by giving in to your child's separation anxiety), we may forget what's most important.

The Good

During our initial consultation, it's not surprising that most parents dwell on the drawbacks of their child's separation anxiety. It's easy to become preoccupied with how much family life is disrupted. But what regularly amazes us is that they always find time to reflect about their child's good qualities. These parents have kept their perspective and realize what's most important—

having a loving, sweet, and affectionate child. Research also suggests that anxious youth tend to be brighter and more creative than the average child. Are you not blessed with a child with these qualities?

"The good" also refers to the good in you. Taking the step to purchase this book tells us that you are sensitive to your child's signals. Being open to our ideas and willing to take the time to implement our program tells us that you care deeply for your child and will do anything in your power to help him. Your child is lucky to have you.

The Healthy

For now, let's focus on the positive features of your child's sensitivity. After all, when all is said and done, your child will still be loving and kind. Let's also assume that your child is not intentionally pushing your buttons but is experiencing genuine anxiety and feeling overwhelmed. Remember, it's not about winning or losing. Your authority is not at stake, no matter how hard your child may try to exert control. And the sooner that you realize that you have nothing to prove, the sooner your child's struggles will feel less personal. Letting go of the desire to control will help you view your child's separation anxiety in a healthy way. By doing so, you have greatly improved your child's chances for overcoming this problem. But before we proceed, we must also discuss how you respond to your separation-anxious child's behavior.

YOUR RESPONSE

You have accomplished so much already in this chapter. You have identified the parenting styles that may be accompanying your child's separation anxiety, and you are working on viewing your child's separation anxiety in a healthier way. Now it's time to discuss the different ways that parents can respond to their separation-anxious child's behavior.

The Attention Factor

It's not surprising that we give children attention when they misbehave or act fearful. We may respond in positive or negative ways (reassurance or reprimand) depending on how we view our child's behaviors (as genuine or manipulative).

The problem is that positive and negative responses to our child's less-than-desirable behaviors actually make them worse. That's right. The general rule of behavior change is to only give your child attention for those behaviors that you wish to see more frequently.

For example, when a child is playing quietly or working independently, such behavior does not seem to require our attention. What do we do? We usually ignore these positive efforts. The general rule of behavior change, however, is to ignore those behaviors that you wish to weaken. Something is not right here. Our intuitive response, "don't fix what isn't broken," tends to strengthen fearful/inappropriate behaviors and weaken positive ones. It's time to turn this around and learn how to shape your child's behavior.

Shape Your Child's Behavior

The idea behind shaping is to give your child maximal positive attention (praise) for behaving appropriately and minimal attention for inappropriate/fearful behaviors. Your approval and (positive) attention is your child's most powerful reward.

At this point, your child is likely receiving too much attention (positive or negative) for separation-anxious behaviors. If you suddenly withdraw your attention, he will initially try harder to get the attention he is accustomed to. It may seem like the situation is getting worse at first. But actually, these efforts are your child's way of telling you that he is unhappy that you're ignoring him.

For example, think of a one-year-old baby boy crying in his crib in the middle of the night. The baby may keep crying until we pick him up. If we pick him up (while still crying), he may learn that continued crying will result in getting picked up. The problem is that the baby is not learning how to fall asleep on his own. But if we gradually wait for longer periods to check on him (without picking up), he will initially cry harder, then eventually learn to fall asleep on his own.

The same is true regarding shaping your child's behavior. First, pay attention to and praise your child's efforts to cope with separation anxiety. Second, let your child know that you understand he is scared but don't give attention to fearful behaviors. For example, if your child is afraid to stay in his room alone, you could say something like, "I know you're afraid to stay in your room alone, but I cannot talk with you until you are calm." Be sure to use a calm, neutral voice.

The next step, of course, is to do your best to ignore your child's fearful/inappropriate behaviors. This is the hard part. That's because before your child's behavior improves, it's likely to get a lot worse. Like the crying baby, your separation-anxious child will protest. But remember, his protest is a natural part of the process. Expect it. Do your best to view this behavior as resulting from genuine anxiety rather than as manipulation.

Modeling Behavior

Your family environment may play a role in sustaining your child's separation anxiety. For example, Kate (protector) modeled fearful behavior for Lenore in several ways. First, because of her own anxiety, she avoided both crowded malls and highways. Second, she showed Kate how she passively got around facing her fears by taking the back roads. Third, and most importantly, she would tell Kate to sleep in her own room but would show her daughter a worried face when making this suggestion, a face that said, "If you get scared, you can stay with me." Which message was Lenore more likely to listen to?

We understand. It's not easy to see our kids get anxious. The loving and protective parent in all of us wants to immediately remove their discomfort. But remember, the only way your child will conquer separation anxiety is if he confronts and feels the fear. To help, you have to reveal through your body language and facial expressions that you're confident that he can cope with separation-related confrontations. Of course, however you feel on the inside (worried) is fine. We suggest you share these feelings and concerns with your spouse or partner.

Please take a moment to complete our end-of-chapter learning check. At the end of the program, complete this learning check again to see if your views of your child have changed.

LEARNING CHECK: UNDERSTANDING MY CHILD'S BEHAVIOR

Circle all that apply

My parenting style most closely resembles the:

Peacekeeper Negotiator Protector Evaluator

My child acts in fearful/inappropriate ways because of the:

Bad (manipulative)	Ugly (oppositional)	Good (sensitive)

When my child experiences separation anxiety, I often respond with:

Positive attention (reassurance)	Negative attention (reprimands)	No attention (ignore)

When my child experiences separation anxiety, I often respond as a:

Fearful model Angry model Passive model Coping model

Summary

Remember, there is no good or bad parenting style. Our objective is to help you recognize how your parenting style affects your separation-anxious child's behavior. You should be thinking about whether you need to make more or fewer active efforts to help your child confront his separation anxiety. At the same time, it's important to view your child's separation anxiety in a healthy way (as resulting from genuine anxiety) and to pay attention to your own behavior during separation-related situations. You should also begin to shape your child's behavior by giving him less attention for fearful/inappropriate behaviors (verbal and nonverbal) and more attention (praise) for positive behaviors/coping efforts. Don't forget to expect some resistance.

Now it's time to take stock of your child's separation anxiety. In chapter 4, using our real-life stories as examples, we'll help you develop specific action plans so your child or adolescent can effectively confront his anxiety.

Chapter 4

Taking Stock

When is Mom coming home? [Looks at watch.] *She said she would be back in fifteen minutes.* [Paces back and forth.] *What if something happened to her?* [Starts to cry then runs toward the phone.]

—Mark

CHAPTER OBJECTIVES

In this chapter you will learn:

- How to develop separation-fears lists (exposures) for each type of separation anxiety using our real-life examples
- How to create a list of your child's safety needs
- How to use our safety-signal selector

DEVELOPING AN ACTION PLAN

In chapter 2, we discussed the four types of separation anxiety and the safety needs that accompany them. Now it's time to develop a specific action plan to help your child gradually confront her separation anxiety.

This action plan will provide you with a series of steps to follow to begin to plan your child's exposures to the situations that she is afraid of. An exposure is when you ask your child to confront a situation that she is either avoiding or enduring with a great deal of anxiety. Remember, in order to conquer her separation anxiety, your child will need to confront and feel the fear. First we will review the real-life examples presented in chapter 2 to help you decide which type(s) of separation anxiety your child may be experiencing. Following each case review, we will present lists of separation fears and safety needs that are relevant to that particular case. The list of separation fears will include all of the situations that the child has difficulty confronting or completely avoids. Then we will ask you to prepare a similar separation-fears list for your child, based on your family's experiences. Once that is complete, we will provide a list of the safety-signal needs for the same real-life example. Again, safety signals are those people, places, objects, or actions that make one feel less scared in an anxiety-provoking situation. After reviewing the list of safety needs for the real-life example, we'll ask you to prepare a similar list of safety needs for your child.

Once your separation-fears and safety-needs lists are completed, we will present our safety-signal selector. The safety-signal selector will help you examine the different dimensions of your child's safety needs. Remember, we want the exposures to gradually increase in the degree of anxiety that your child experiences. You will be able to make initial exposures less anxiety provoking and more likely to be successful by referring to the safety-signal selector. You will also be able to make later exposures more challenging.

Your first step in formulating a good action plan is to go through the following real-life case examples and read each, even if you think you already know what type of separation anxiety your child is experiencing. Reviewing each type of anxiety is valuable because many children exhibit features of more than one type. This way the lists of safety needs and separation fears you eventually construct for your child will reflect an accurate variety of situations. These lists will be an important element of the action plan you will create by the end of this chapter. Let's begin with Debbie's example.

Debbie's Example

Debbie follows her mother, Janice, because of a fear that something bad will happen to Debbie when she's alone. She's what we call a follower. Debbie needs someone to monitor her whereabouts (a medical monitor) just in case she becomes sick. Let's take a look at the separation-fears list that could serve as possible exposures for Debbie.

DEBBIE'S SEPARATION-FEARS LIST (FOLLOWER)

STAYING ALONE:

- Bedroom
- Living room or kitchen (where Debbie does homework alone)
- Downstairs playroom
- Bathroom

LEAVING JANICE ALONE (NO FOLLOWING):

- Doing the laundry
- Throwing out the garbage
- Talking on the phone
- Going to the bathroom

Now, we're ready for you to list your child's separation fears. To help you get started, let's think of all the specific places in your home that you would like your child to be able to spend time in alone. Second, consider activities that you would like to be able to accomplish without being followed. Now, let's list the actual situations that are anxiety provoking for your child.

YOUR CHILD'S SEPARATION-FEARS LIST (FOLLOWER)

SITUATIONS:

1: ____________________

2: ____________________

3: ____________________

4: ____________________

5: ____________________

Now let's take a closer look at Debbie's safety needs and safety signals.

DEBBIE'S SAFETY NEEDS (MEDICAL MONITOR)

Safe Persons: Janice and Ray (younger brother)

Safe Objects: video games, television, drink/food

Safe Actions: following, eliciting parental promises (check on her)

Safe Places: Any room with Janice or Ray or others (father, friend)

Debbie's safety needs are representative of children with daytime fears of being alone at home when other family members are somewhere in the house. As you might expect, her strongest safety needs are safe persons and safe actions. Safe places are typically more important for children with abandonment fears (like Peter). Take a moment to list your child's safety needs. Use the learning check that you completed in chapter 2 as a guide.

Safe Persons: ______________________________

Safe Objects: ______________________________

Safe Actions: ______________________________

Safe Places: ______________________________

SAFETY-SIGNAL SELECTION

The next step is to examine our safety-signal selector to determine how to make Debbie's exposures gradually more challenging. Let's take a look at figure 4.1.

As you can see from the figure, there are many dimensions along which we can make changes to an exposure to make it more or less challenging. For example, your child may be able to stay alone in a room as long as she can see you. But, if you were to move out of sight (varying distance), your child might feel much more anxious. We will return to the safety-signal selector in chapter 6 to show you how it can be used to guide you in planning your child's exposures. For now, let's consider the safety-signal selector in relation to Debbie.

As long as Debbie has *access* to Janice or Ray she will feel safe (this is one of her safety needs). We can make Debbie's exposures more challenging by gradually increasing the *distance* of her safe persons. For example, at first Debbie may be willing to stay in her bedroom alone as long as Janice or Ray is within sight (for instance, in the hallway). She may also allow her safe persons to move further away if she can hear them. Naturally, having her safe persons move to other locations, such as a different floor, will be more difficult. In chapter 6, using Debbie as our example, we'll show you how to help your child overcome her fear of being alone using our step-by-step plans.

Safety-Signal Selector

ACCESS to safety signals

person place object action

DURATION of exposure

under 5 minutes	up to 30 minutes	no time limit

DISTANCE from home, place, or person

within sight	within sound	neither

FAMILIARITY of situation, place, or person

familiar unfamiliar

PLANNING of exposure

well in advance	short notice	unexpected

TIMING of exposure

day night

Figure 4.1: Safety-Signal Selector

Lenore's Example

Lenore sleeps in her parent's bed because she fears that an intruder will break into the house (she frequently "visits" her parents at night). She needs her mother, Kate, to serve as a security guard at night, protecting her from intruders. As we take a look at the separation-fears list that could serve as possible exposures for Lenore, you will notice that Lenore's separation-fears list looks different than Debbie's list. As you remember, Debbie is afraid of being alone anywhere in the house, and she follows her mother around as Janice completes a variety of needed chores/activities. Thus, Debbie's separation-fears list consisted of different places to stay alone and different activities for her mother to complete. Lenore's separation anxiety is primarily centered around where and with whom she sleeps. Therefore, her separation-fears list consists of different scenarios, all involving staying in her bedroom in the evening.

LENORE'S SEPARATION-FEARS LIST (VISITOR)

STAYING IN HER BEDROOM (AT NIGHT):

- After dinner (alone)
- Getting ready for bed
- Trying to fall asleep
- If awakens during the night

In our experience, three nighttime scenarios are common for children that fear sleeping alone:

- Your child is sleeping in your bedroom regularly.

- You are sleeping or spending much of the night in your child's bedroom.
- Your child is frequently visiting your bedroom at night (stays in your bedroom or you end up staying in her bedroom).

YOUR CHILD'S SEPARATION-FEARS LIST (VISITOR)

SITUATIONS:

1: ______________________________

2: ______________________________

3: ______________________________

4: ______________________________

5: ______________________________

Let's take a closer look at Lenore's safety needs and safety signals.

LENORE'S SAFETY NEEDS (SECURITY GUARD)

Safe Persons: Kate

Safe Objects: Night-light, Kate's pillow or comforter

Safe Actions: Promises and/or reassurances (that she can sleep in her parent's room)

Safe Places: Parental bedroom

Lenore's safety needs are representative of older children and adolescents that fear sleeping alone. Younger children may also have difficulty being alone (at night) in other places as well, such as the bathroom. Fears of sleeping alone are largely about having access to safe persons. Lenore did not view her father, Jack, as a safe person. He often slept through the night and was neither sensitive to Lenore's signals nor her separation anxiety. Please take a moment to list your child's safety needs. Use the learning check in chapter 2 as your guide.

Safe Persons: ________________________________

Safe Objects: ________________________________

Safe Actions: ________________________________

Safe Places: ________________________________

SAFETY-SIGNAL SELECTION

Let's return to the safety-signal selector to determine how to make Lenore's exposures more challenging while still helping her to feel reasonably secure.

As long as Lenore has *access* to Kate, she will feel safe. We can make Lenore's exposures more challenging by gradually changing the *distance* of her safe persons. For example, as a first step, after dinner, we'll have Lenore stay in her room alone as we change Kate's distance from her (moving from hallway, bathroom, to kitchen). This step will help prepare Lenore to stay alone during the more challenging nighttime routine.

Regarding this routine, we'll proceed carefully to help Lenore continue to feel more secure. For example, Kate could initially agree to stay with Lenore (in her bedroom) for the entire night. As Lenore feels more secure, we can gradually vary Kate's distance (staying in hallway, etc.) and the *duration* of time that Lenore spends alone in her bedroom. Ultimately, we want Lenore to be able to fall asleep after Kate leaves her bedroom. We'll show you how to accomplish this goal with your child using our step-by-step plans in chapter 6.

Peter's Example

Peter is very sensitive to the physical feelings in his body and fears he will get sick. These gloomy expectations are why we refer to him as the misfortune teller. Because he's worried about stomach upset, he is afraid to eat before or during school as well as at other people's houses. Peter also feels uncomfortable outside of his home unless he has access to safe persons or safe objects that he perceives will protect him from serious illness (lifeguards). Let's take a look at the separation-fears list that could serve as possible exposures for Peter.

PETER'S SEPARATION-FEARS LIST (MISFORTUNE TELLER)

EATING-RELATED ACTIVITIES:

- Breakfast (before school)
- Lunch (school cafeteria)
- Dinner (outside of the home)

SOCIAL ACTIVITIES:

- Mall
- Movie

As you can see, similar situations for Peter will be more challenging simply by changing his safe persons or the familiarity of situations. This is likely to be the case for your child or adolescent as well.

YOUR CHILD'S SEPARATION-FEARS LIST (MISFORTUNE TELLER)

SITUATIONS:

1: ____

2: ____

3: ____

4: ____

5: ____

Your child or adolescent's fear of getting sick may not involve a fear of eating. But our experience suggests that the stronger the fear of getting sick, the more likely that (a lack of) eating will be involved. What's most important here, however, is to identify events that your child or adolescent is reluctant to attend because of the possibility of getting sick. For now, let's take a closer look to see how Peter's safety signals and safety needs affect his separation anxiety.

PETER'S SAFETY NEEDS (LIFEGUARD)

Safe Persons: Rick, Mary, school nurse, best friend, baseball coach

Safe Objects: Water bottle

Safe Actions: Calling a parent, staying close to a friend, school nurse, or baseball coach

Safe Places: Home, nurse's office, public bathroom

Peter's separation fears are directly related to having *access* to safe persons and safe places. When these safety needs are unavailable, Peter may still be willing to attend activities away from home if he has access to safe objects or actions. He needs assurances that some object (water bottle) will prevent physical illness or that he can get in touch with someone (mother) if necessary. Please take a moment to list your child or adolescent's safety needs. Once again, use the learning check in chapter 2 as your guide.

Safe Persons: ____

Safe Objects: ____

Safe Actions: ____

Safe Places: ____

SAFETY-SIGNAL SELECTION

Let's take another look at the safety-signal selector to determine how to make Peter's exposures gradually more challenging while still protecting his sense of security. If we left it up to Peter, he wouldn't eat his breakfast or lunch and would rarely socialize with his friends outside of school-related activities.

For example, we can start by encouraging Peter to eat minimal amounts of breakfast (maybe a half a bagel, glass of milk or juice) before school simply to show him that he will not become sick. The amount that he eats is not important as long as he eats or drinks something. As he progresses, we can gradually encourage him to eat small portions in the school cafeteria and then at other people's homes. We can also encourage Peter to attend social activities, first with family, then friends. We'll show you how to accomplish these goals with your child, using Peter as our example, with our step-by-step plans in chapter 7.

Mark's Example

Mark's abandonment fears stem from worry that something terrible (like a car accident) will happen to his mother, Peggy, when he is separated from her. He watches the minutes when he's separated from Peggy, so we call him the timekeeper. Mark refuses to attend social and extracurricular events and strongly resists Peggy's attempts to leave the house without him, acting as her effective bodyguard. Let's take a look at the separation-fears list that could serve as possible exposures for Mark.

MARK'S SEPARATION-FEARS LIST (TIMEKEEPER)

SCHOOL-RELATED SITUATIONS:

- Taking the bus to school
- Taking the bus home
- Attending field trips

SOCIAL SITUATIONS:

- Playdates
- Birthday parties
- Karate class
- Sleepovers

LETTING PEGGY LEAVE THE HOUSE (NO TIMEKEEPING):

- Going shopping
- Socializing with friends (during the evening)

Mark's abandonment fears are all about his mother, Peggy. If Mark cannot be with her, he needs to know that Peggy is safe. Mark may be willing to attend social/extracurricular events as long as he can see his mother for the entire time, knows his mother's precise whereabouts, or can call her at any given moment.

YOUR CHILD'S SEPARATION-FEARS LIST (TIMEKEEPER)

SITUATIONS:

1: ____________________

2: ____________________

3: ____________________

4: ____________________

5: ____________________

Now, let's take a closer look at Mark's safety needs and safety signals.

MARK'S SAFETY NEEDS (PARENTAL BODYGUARD)

Safe Persons: Peggy

Safe Objects: Peggy's car keys, pocketbook

Safe Actions: Peggy promising to stay home (during the school day), Peggy staying with Mark (during social/extracurricular event), Peggy promising to be home on time (in evening), Mark making unlimited phone calls to Peggy's cell phone

Safe Places: Anywhere with Peggy

Please take a moment to list your child or adolescent's safety needs. Use the learning check in chapter 2 as your guide.

Safe Persons: ______________________________

Safe Objects: ______________________________

Safe Actions: ______________________________

Safe Places: ______________________________

SAFETY-SIGNAL SELECTION

Let's take one more look at the safety-signal selector to determine how to make Mark's exposures more challenging by gradually changing access/distance to Peggy while still helping him to feel more secure.

As a first step, we want Mark to start attending social/extracurricular events. This may only happen if Peggy stays for the entire time during each new event. As Mark feels more comfortable, we can gradually remove Peggy's presence and add in some of Mark's safe actions to preserve his security. Our ultimate goal, of course, is to have Mark attend these events with minimal safe actions (perhaps just an emergency phone call, if needed).

When Mark becomes comfortable separating, we can then encourage Peggy to go shopping and to visit with friends without him. Once again, we'll initially allow Mark to depend heavily on his safe actions to get through the exposures. As his confidence builds, we'll gradually eliminate his safety needs and replace them with coping tools. We'll show you how to accomplish these goals with your child, using Mark as our example, with our step-by-step plans in chapter 7.

Summary

In this chapter, we helped you take stock of your child's separation anxiety. You now have a separation-fears list and an exposure plan for your child. More importantly, you understand how to use our safety-signal selector to challenge your child while still retaining her security. But before we show you how to effectively carry out these plans (chapters 6 and 7), you will need to empower your child with some coping skills.

Chapter 5

Empowering Your Child with Coping Skills

Debbie, does having a stomachache mean that anything bad will happen to you?

—Janice

What are the chances that someone will break into our house tonight, Lenore?

—Kate

CHAPTER OBJECTIVES

In this chapter you will learn:

- How to help your child think like a problem solver in separation-related situations
- How to help your child use cognitive therapy techniques as coping skills
- How to help your child use relaxation exercises as coping skills
- How to help your child stay motivated throughout the program

HELPING YOUR CHILD COPE

In chapter 4, you developed an effective list of exposures for your child that is designed to protect his sense of security. Yet, no matter how hard you try, your child will still become anxious when confronting separation-related situations. Believe it or not, *thinking* about separation-related situations is much more upsetting than any actual incidents.

For example, think about the last time that you became lost on your way to an important social event. What thoughts immediately popped into your head? Did you worry that you would never find the place? That you'd be the last one to arrive? Did you consider just giving up and driving home? Well, what actually happened? Chances are, everything turned out fine. In fact, you probably weren't the last one to arrive. However, if you gave in to your worries and drove home, in your mind, showing up for the event would have been a disaster.

It's important to keep in mind that such disasters rarely come true. In fact, even when situations turn sour, their outcomes are usually not half as bad as we had anticipated. It's the same for your child's worries about separation. So, in this chapter, we are going to present three lessons that will help you teach your child coping skills that he will need to begin to confront anxiety-provoking situations. Our first lesson is to help your child think like a problem solver by learning to identify and change his separation-anxious thoughts.

LESSON 1: DISASTER RELIEF BY CHANGING THOUGHTS

Let's think for a moment about the list of exposures you put together for your child in chapter 4. You may have written down that you'd like your child to be able to go on a playdate alone, or sleep alone in his own bed, or even to be able to eat breakfast before going to school. What do you think would happen if you told your child that you would like him to complete that exposure right now? Your child might have a temper tantrum, cry, or even become sick to his stomach. You may think that this is going to be an impossible task. But, we're missing a very important step before we can request that your child complete even the least anxiety-provoking exposure. We need to empower your child with new coping skills that will make it possible for him to confront feared situations.

Let's think again about that time that you may have gotten lost on the way to a social event. What was it that made you feel most anxious? It was probably the thoughts that popped into your head, telling you that it was going to be a disaster. It's the same for your separation-anxious child when he becomes anxious about an impending separation. The thoughts that pop into his head, for example, "Mom might not pick me up," turn a simple social event into a potential disaster. So, before we can ask your child to confront such a feared event, we need to help him with these thoughts.

In this lesson, we are going to present a series of steps to help you teach your child how to identify, tolerate, and then finally challenge these thoughts that are increasing his avoidance of feared situations. You will learn how to ask your child particular questions that will teach him how to develop alternative explanations for his fearful thoughts and how to develop healthier coping thoughts. Let's get started.

Step 1: Identifying Automatic Thoughts

The first step in helping your separation-anxious child to cope more effectively is identifying his automatic (unrealistic) thoughts. Automatic thoughts are our brain's way of telling us that we're anxious. Without warning, these thoughts pop into our heads, make us feel uncomfortable, and tell us to run away from the anxiety-provoking event as fast as possible.

We often believe that these thoughts are true. As adults, intellectually, we can sometimes dismiss them, but children are more likely to feel as if these thoughts are true and act on them. This reaction is problematic since automatic thoughts are often based on little or no evidence. Let's take a look at the relationship between situations, feelings, and automatic thoughts using our real-life stories.

DEBBIE'S EXAMPLE

Situation: Being alone during the day

Feeling: Scared, stomachache

Thoughts: Something bad will happen

As long as Debbie's mother, Janice, and younger brother, Ray, continue to be her medical monitors, Debbie will feel safe and not have negative automatic thoughts about bad things that may happen. However, if Debbie is left alone, her automatic thoughts will have her believe that something bad will occur.

LENORE'S EXAMPLE

Situation: Being alone at night

Feeling: Apprehensive

Thoughts: What if someone breaks into the house?

As long as Kate continues to be Lenore's security guard, Lenore will not have any automatic thoughts about an intruder. However, Lenore believes that if she had stayed in her bedroom alone, someone would have broken into the house.

PETER'S EXAMPLE

Situation: Going to school or an event after school

Feeling: Stomachache (feeling sick)

Thoughts: What if I throw up? What if I can't get help?

As long as Peter continues to stay nearby a lifeguard (a parent, friend, nurse, or coach), he will have minimal automatic thoughts. But in Peter's mind, if he went to school or an extracurricular event without having access to these safe people, he would have gotten sick.

MARK'S EXAMPLE

Situation: Waiting for Peggy to come home or getting picked up from a social event

Feeling: Worried

Thoughts: What if Mom forgets to pick me up? What if Mom gets killed in a car accident?

If your child is like Mark, he may refuse to go places unless you promise to stay home, remain at the event, or pick him up on time. As long as Peggy allows Mark to be her parental bodyguard, Mark has minimal feelings of anxiety or automatic thoughts. But if Peggy is late, Mark would assume something terrible happened to his mom.

What do the parents in our real-life stories have in common? Like you, they love their children and want to protect them from experiencing distress. But remember, your child needs to feel the fear, and this means that he must learn to tolerate the automatic thoughts that promote it. You can help your child do this through the power of reflection.

Step 2: Tolerating Automatic Thoughts

Now that your child can identify his automatic thoughts, we need to teach him how to tolerate those thoughts. Tolerating the thoughts means understanding that it's okay to have fearful thoughts, even if they make you uncomfortable. Remember that in order for your child to conquer his fear, he is going to have to confront and feel the anxiety. That means he will need to get used to the feeling of anxiety while making sure that the anxiety doesn't keep him from doing the things he wants. You may wonder, how can you possibly teach your child to tolerate fearful thoughts? What can you do when he repeatedly asks you questions that you have already answered, for example, "What if you're late picking me up?" We're going to show you how to ask your child particular questions (called *reflection*) that will allow him to use the information he already has to reassure himself, rather than you reassuring him that there is nothing to worry about.

Let's take a look at the following example in which Peggy uses simple reflection rather than reassurance to help Mark think about his separation anxiety.

Mark: Mom, you're staying home today while I'm in school, right?

Peggy: What have I told you?

Mark: Please tell me again.

Peggy: Do you really need to ask me?

Mark: Please!

Peggy: I think you already know the answer.

Mark knows his mother will stay home, yet he will feel uncomfortable (experience automatic thoughts about it) until his mother reassures him. The idea is to help your child get accustomed to experiencing some discomfort. Your child's tolerance for such a scenario will depend on his temperament (strong willed versus passive), intensity, and willingness to feel uncomfortable. If your child becomes too upset, consider enforcing a three-question limit. Here, you can still reassure your child ("Yes, I will stay home") but only three times in any given situation. Practice reflection until your child accepts that you will now be using reassurance to a minimal degree. At that point, you will be ready to help your child challenge his automatic thoughts.

Step 3: Challenging Automatic Thoughts

Until now, your child has accepted his automatic thoughts at face value. Telling him that nothing bad will happen may only temporarily make him feel better. In fact, your child may not believe you since he still feels uncomfortable.

Your child needs to learn that there is no truth to his automatic thoughts, and this shift will only happen by getting through separation-related confrontations unharmed. But your child may not attempt any exposures until he believes there is a good chance that nothing bad will happen to either one of you. It's time to shatter the myth of the separation-anxiety phantom by helping your child examine the evidence regarding his past separation-related experiences.

THE SEPARATION ANXIETY PHANTOM

Your child's separation-anxious thoughts are very much like a phantom—a presence always lurking in the background telling him that something bad will happen. Let's dispel the myth of the separation-anxiety phantom by developing your child's private investigation skills. This can be accomplished by asking your child a series of questions that are based on commonly used cognitive therapy techniques (Beck 1995). These questions will help you and your child gather evidence supporting or disproving his automatic thoughts.

- Has (the feared event) ever happened in the past?
- If so, when was the last time it happened?
- How many times has it happened?
- If (the feared event) happened, how bad was it?

Your goal is to help your child recognize that what his fearful automatic thoughts tell him will happen actually has minimal or no likelihood of occurring. We illustrate with the following dialogue between Lenore and her mother, Kate.

Lenore: What if someone breaks into the house tonight?

Kate: Has that ever happened before?

Lenore: Never [sighs]. But it might.

Kate: What are the real chances that someone will break into our house tonight?

Lenore: A good chance.

Kate: But didn't you say that no one has ever broken into the house before?

Lenore: Yeah . . .

Kate: So, what do you think the real chances are?

Lenore: Not very much.

Kate: That sounds about right.

Notice that by examining the evidence of the past, Kate helped Lenore think about the future likelihood of feared events. Lenore now has a more realistic understanding of the likelihood of anyone breaking into her house. This is a step in the right direction. Remember, she used to think that it was very likely that there would be a break-in, every night. Now she understands that it is an unlikely event. But, we still have more work to do because Lenore is still terrified. The separation-anxiety phantom defies logic. Even though she *knows* a break-in is unlikely, Lenore's automatic thoughts still make her *feel* like someone will break in.

It's important to keep in mind that thinking realistically does not come naturally to separation-anxious youth. They are much more used to thinking about disastrous scenarios. It is only by repeatedly challenging her automatic thoughts, and at the same time finding out that nothing bad will happen to her, that Lenore will begin to believe that there's no truth to her automatic thoughts. Thus, while helping your child have a more realistic understanding of the likelihood of events is an important part of challenging automatic thoughts, there is more involved. The next step is to help your child understand the circumstances surrounding separation-anxious events.

UNDERSTANDING THE BIG PICTURE

Lenore knows that it is unlikely that someone will break into her house. Yet, she still worries. To her, every nighttime noise means that someone is trying to break in. For this reason, we need to put Lenore's separation fears in a larger context. We need to get her to think not only about her experiences in her own home, but to broaden her thinking to the experiences of other people she knows. For example, Kate could ask her the following questions:

- Do you personally know of any robberies or break-ins?
- Has anyone in the neighborhood ever been robbed?
- Have any of your friends ever been robbed?

This type of questioning helps Lenore recognize that it is unlikely for her or anyone else she knows to be the victim of a robbery or break-in. Of course, if your child's separation fears have even remotely come true in the past, we have to take a step further and help him understand what actually happened.

For example, Peter did throw up once several years ago, but this was the result of a stomach virus. Nevertheless, every time Peter feels uncomfortable, he thinks he is about to become ill. We can expand our questioning as follows:

- How many times have you thought/felt you were going to be sick? (hundreds)
- How many times have you actually been sick? (once)
- Does feeling sick mean you will be sick? (no)
- What's usually the underlying feeling beneath your queasy stomach? (anxiety)

At this point, your child may begin to believe that it is unlikely that the bad thing he fears will happen will actually come about. However, he still needs to learn to think about more realistic and safe outcomes.

Step 4: Developing Alternative Explanations

Mark is convinced that if his mother, Peggy, comes home late from an outing, something terrible has happened to her. It's not enough that he understands that such an event is unlikely. As unlikely as it is, Mark is still afraid because he knows he would be devastated without his mom. How would he cope if it happened? In the following example, Peggy helps Mark seek alternative explanations for her possible lateness in arriving home.

Peggy: Have I ever come home late?

Mark: [Worried look] Yes . . . and don't ever do it again.

Peggy: What do you mean?

Mark: You told Daddy and me you were coming home at 9:00 P.M. last week.

Peggy: But you weren't supposed to be waiting up for me.

Mark: You were late!

Peggy: Did anything bad happen to me?

Mark: [Shakes his head.]

Peggy: Does Mommy ever forget to call?

Mark: When you're out with your friends.

Peggy: So, if I ever come home late, what probably happened?

Mark: I don't know.

Peggy: It means I was . . .

Mark: Having fun with your friends?

Peggy: That's right. Can you remember to tell yourself that, if this happens again?

Mark: I'll try.

Peggy: Good.

Following much practice of the four steps, your child will be less likely to panic when thinking about separation-anxious events. However, for him to willingly confront separation-related situations, he will need to develop some coping thoughts.

Step 5: Developing Coping Thoughts

Given that separation-anxious children tend to focus on negative outcomes, it would make sense to help them think more positively. But positive thoughts rarely help children cope.

For example, if your child does poorly on tests, rather than thinking "I will do poorly," he or she could think, "I will do well." But such a strategy is not reassuring since it's not based on actual evidence. Coping thoughts, on the other hand, are constructive ways of thinking about how to handle difficult situations. For example, that child who did poorly on a test might say to himself, "If I get extra help or study harder, I will probably do better on the test." You can help your child develop coping thoughts by asking him evidence-based questions while encouraging healthy answers. We illustrate this process with Mark and Lenore.

MARK'S EXAMPLE

Situation: Mark is waiting for his mother to come home.

Automatic thought: What if Mom was in an accident?

Coping thoughts:

1. Is there any evidence that this is true? *No.*
2. What has mostly likely happened? *She's stuck in traffic.*
3. What's a coping thought that will help? *My mom is always fine.*
4. What is the best thing that could end up happening? *Mom could even come home early.*

LENORE'S EXAMPLE

Situation: One hour before bedtime.

Automatic thought: What if someone breaks into the house?

Coping thoughts:

1. Is there any evidence that this will happen? *No.*
2. What is most likely to happen? *I might hear the wind howling or the heat banging, but it won't be a burglar.*
3. What's a coping thought that will help? *I can stay alone . . . I'll try to sleep alone.*
4. What is the best thing that could end up happening? *I'll fall asleep and not be scared at all.*

The idea is to practice this process until your child can readily think this way on his own. It's often helpful to ask your child, "What's the best thing that could happen?" Such a strategy steers them away from emphasizing negative or catastrophic outcomes. Our goal is to help your child visualize coping rather than succumbing to his worst fears.

Now, we're getting closer to helping your child get ready to confront separation-anxious situations. But we still need to help him learn to calm down, especially if he fears getting sick. This brings us to our next lesson.

LESSON 2: CALMING THE STORM WITH RELAXATION EXERCISES

Now that your child can identify and challenge his automatic thoughts and is on his way to developing healthy coping skills, is he ready to confront separation-anxious scenarios? Probably not quite yet. First we need to look at the physical feelings he may be experiencing when faced with anxiety-provoking situations. In this lesson we will help you examine whether your child is experiencing physical feelings such as stomachaches or difficulty breathing when he is anxious. If so, we'll show you how to help him become aware of and learn to tolerate these physical feelings. In addition, you'll learn how to help your child relax with deep breathing and deep muscle relaxation exercises. Finally, you'll be able to help your child develop a plan for using these relaxation skills to feel more in control when he is anxious.

Step 1: Understanding Physical Feelings

The first step is to help your child understand his physical feelings during separation-related situations. Common physical feelings include stomachaches, headaches, dizziness, difficulty breathing, or simply just feeling uncomfortable. Young children, like Debbie, typically experience stomachaches or feel uncomfortable. Adolescents like Peter may experience more full-fledged physical feelings and a fear of becoming sick. It's important to keep in mind that some children may not experience these feelings at all. Rather, like Lenore and Mark, they are primarily worriers. Of course, others experience both worry and physical feelings. Your goals are to help your child understand our "Triple A's":

- **A**nticipate physical feelings during separation-related situations

- **A**ccept physical feelings (rather than be afraid) as a normal part of experiencing anxiety
- **A**ppreciate the lack of connection between physical feelings and actual illness

First, it's important to help your child learn to expect these physical feelings in situations that make him feel anxious. If he expects to feel sick to his stomach in the morning while he's getting ready for school, he may feel less scared when he first notices the feelings. Your child also needs to learn to tell himself that the physical feelings are just part of the way that he experiences his anxiety. And finally, your child needs to understand that his physical feelings are not a result of real physical illness. Over time, he will be able to recognize that he feels nauseated in the morning because he is anxious about going to school. Once he accomplishes that, he will be less likely to worry about getting ill in school.

Let's look at the following example, where Janice helps Debbie make the connection between her physical feelings and separation anxiety.

Janice: Debbie, go ahead and finish your homework here at the kitchen table. I'll be right back.

Debbie: [Scared expression.]

Janice: I have to put the laundry in the dryer.

Debbie: [Stands up, holds her stomach, then grabs Janice's hand.]

Janice: Are you scared?

Debbie: [Nods.]

Janice: How come?

Debbie: My tummy . . . [Holds her stomach.]

Janice: Please sit down.

Debbie: [Cries] I can't . . .

Janice: Do you often get stomachaches when I have to leave you?

Debbie: Uh huh.

Janice: Is it okay to have a stomachache if you're scared?

Debbie: I guess.

Janice: Does having a stomachache mean that anything bad will happen to you?

Debbie: No?

Janice: Did you need me to sit with you to do your homework?

Debbie: I guess not.

Janice: Will you let me go down to the laundry room by myself next time?

Debbie: I'll try [smiles weakly].

Step 2: Tolerating Physical Feelings

In Lesson 1 (Step 2), the idea was to help your child tolerate his automatic thoughts. Similarly, in this step, we want your child to accept his physical feelings rather than avoid them. In many cases, the thoughts and physical feelings are naturally connected. This was certainly true for Peter. Simply thinking about eating breakfast before school triggered his fear of getting sick. In the following example, Peter's mother, Mary, encourages him to do just that.

Mary: Peter, could you eat something for breakfast before school?

Peter: [Looks surprised] I don't know . . .

Mary: How about half a bagel?

Peter: But . . . I never eat . . . before school.

Mary: I know. Do you think that's a good idea?

Peter: I guess not.

Mary: Do you sometimes feel light-headed or dizzy in school?

Peter: Sometimes.

Mary: Could it be from not eating anything?

Peter: Maybe.

Mary: You might feel better if you ate something.

Peter: [Doesn't respond.]

Mary: How are you going to know that you won't get sick if you don't even try?

Peter: [Sighs] Okay . . . [Looks at bagel, holds his stomach.]

Simply thinking about eating the bagel is helping Peter learn to tolerate his physical feelings. During his first few attempts, it's not necessary for him to actually eat anything. After practicing the first two steps in this lesson, your child will be eager to learn how to relax. Let's start with deep breathing exercises.

Step 3: Relaxing with Deep Breathing

Think of the last time you were driving on the highway and almost became the victim of a reckless driver's behavior. In that one brief moment, what happened to your breathing? Did it suddenly turn shallow and rapid? If so, did it set off a chain reaction of physical feelings and tension?

Of course, this situation is an extreme example that would elicit panic in almost anyone. But for your separation-anxious child, merely anticipating being alone or abandoned is more than enough to trigger these kind of rapid shallow breaths, called *overbreathing*. For this reason, we recommend teaching your child deep breathing exercises.

Deep breathing is one of the easiest and most effective ways of helping children calm down under stress. This is especially important, since as you know, separation anxiety often escalates quickly. You can help your child relax by having him follow our three-step sequence:

1. Breathe in. Be sure he inhales through his nose slowly and deeply. Count to three out loud so he can follow your pace.

2. Breathe out. Be sure your child blows out through his mouth slowly and gently. Count to three out loud so he can follow your pace.

3. Help him practice the breathing exercises until he can breathe on cue (take a deep breath, breathe out).

PRACTICE YOURSELF

The idea is to breathe in slowly and deeply (effortlessly) through your nose for three seconds. As you breathe in, your chest and belly should expand. When you breathe out, be sure to blow the air through your mouth, slowly and gently, for three seconds. Practice until you have a nice, smooth rhythm and no longer need to count to yourself. Consider practicing during your own stressful situations to develop mastery.

Step 4: Relaxing with Deep Muscle Relaxation

Deep muscle relaxation works well with deep breathing to help protect your separation-anxious child's feeling of security.

Deep muscle relaxation involves first tensing different muscle groups, then relaxing them. The idea is that it's impossible to be both tense and relaxed all at once. Thus, if your child can bring on the relaxation, he will feel more in control. These exercises (based on Ollendick and Cerny 1981) are also an excellent way to help your child cope with anger. You may find these exercises most helpful if your child is strong willed and oppositional, like Debbie or Mark.

Following are the muscle groups that you will be tensing and relaxing. You can have your child practice them all or simply use those groups which your child is most sensitive to (like the stomach). Each muscle group has several possible exercises. Try them out with your child to determine his preferences.

First, demonstrate for your child how to tense and relax for each of the muscle groups. Have your child tense for three seconds, followed by three seconds of relaxation. When your child relaxes, help him let go as completely as possible. Be sure he experiences a sense of calm and relief after each exercise. Keep practicing until your child can perform the exercises on cue when you ask him to.

The idea is that when your child tenses then relaxes his muscles, he will release his anxiety and frustration. After your child relaxes his muscles, help him notice how calm he now feels. Tell him that this is a way he can bring on the relaxation and feel more secure on his own. The ultimate goal is to have your child be able to use these exercises to replace fearful and inappropriate behavior, such as crying or having a tantrum, when faced with situations that make him feel anxious.

HANDS AND ARMS

- Squeeze your fists.
- Show me your muscles (biceps).
- Stretch your arms above your head.

SHOULDERS

- Tense your shoulders.
- Lift your shoulders up to your ears.
- Stretch your arms to your side.

MOUTH

- Press your lips together.
- Open your mouth wide.

STOMACH

- Hold your stomach in.
- Make yourself as thin as you can.
- Tighten up your stomach.

HEAD

- Arch your eyebrows.
- Tighten your nose.
- Make wrinkles on your forehead.

LEGS AND FEET

- Push your feet down on the floor.
- Stretch your legs.
- Curl your toes (upward or downward).

It's helpful to prepare a short script of what you will say before taking your child through the exercises. For instance, for the hands exercises, you could say something like: "Squeeze your hands as tightly as you can. Hold them for three seconds. Hold them tight . . . tight . . . tight. Now release them. Feel your hands go limp."

Step 5: Developing Relaxation Skills

Talk to your child and help him develop his relaxation repertoire. Let him know that he can use breathing and muscle-relaxation exercises when he is becoming anxious, annoyed, or upset. Help your child realize that relaxation is a good way (rather than avoidance) of coping with separation anxiety and anger. Together you can develop a plan consisting of deep breathing followed by two or three of his favorite muscle-relaxation exercises. This will set the stage for helping your child manage real-life separation—anxious confrontations to be discussed in chapters 6 and 7. But before we proceed, we have to address a most important question. Is your child motivated to overcome his separation anxiety? This brings us to our third lesson.

LESSON 3: ENHANCING MOTIVATION WITH REWARDS

Now that your child is aware of his physical feelings and is able to use deep breathing and deep muscle relaxation exercises to decrease his feelings of anxiety, we're ready to think about asking him to start confronting those separation-related situations that he is afraid of. But first, we need to think about how motivated your child is to confront these situations. Some separation-anxious children will be strongly motivated to confront their anxiety because they are so frustrated that their fear prevents them from doing what they want. These children may be ready to forge ahead right now. Other children may not really understand why anything needs to change and may in fact be resistant to change. If your child is like this, you may need a little help in enlisting his full cooperation. In this lesson we'll help you explore whether it might be helpful to include a reward-based component in your child's treatment plan. We'll also demonstrate how to set up an effective reward system, should you so desire.

Step 1: To Reward or Not to Reward?

Think of the last time you accomplished a challenging goal. It may have been for losing weight, exercising regularly, or smoking less. How did you evaluate the outcome?

- Did you reward yourself for a job well done?
- Did you criticize each of your failures along the way?
- Did you simply accept the outcome as something you expected of yourself?

Your child may not understand why he cannot sleep in your room anymore or why you would like to drop him off at a birthday party. The idea that he needs to feel even more anxious to ultimately cope better may not make much sense at first. In fact, he may view you as mean and resist being exposed to separation-related situations.

Prior to reading this book, you may have thought that such an outlook was manipulative. In addition, you may have caught yourself questioning why your child cannot be alone/sleep alone and/or be dropped off at certain places. But now, we hope you have a healthier perspective on your child's behavior. As a result, you recognize that your child's:

- Separation anxiety is genuine and not his fault
- Resistance to experiencing separation anxiety is normal and an expected part of the process

- Temperament (strong willed versus passive) is related to his degree of resistance

For these reasons, and the fact that separation-anxious youth tend to focus on failure, we think you'll agree at least initially to attempt to keep things positive. In this process we emphasize partial successes (small steps) and rewards for a willingness to confront potentially unpleasant separation-related situations.

It's important to keep in mind that a reward is not a bribe. Granting access to a privilege (like watching television) to stop a child's acting-out behaviors is an example of a bribe. We don't feel good about this. In fact, such an arrangement may actually increase the likelihood of a child's inappropriate behavior.

A reward, however, is a positive consequence for a child engaging in a desired behavior. The purpose of a reward is to increase the likelihood of the positive behavior occurring again. A reward may help your child work hard to overcome his separation anxiety. For our purposes, consider this program we've been detailing as your child's job and the resulting rewards his salary. The message that you want to convey to your child is: "I know confronting separation-related situations is hard for you, so if you're willing to try, you should be rewarded."

Of course, not every child will need or benefit from a rewards system. This may be the case if your child only participates in the exposures for the rewards. For now, let's give your child the benefit of the doubt and create a rewards system.

Step 2: Structuring the Rewards System

The idea is not to spend a great deal of money. The rewards system should consist of:

- Small, inexpensive items (for instance, sports cards, stickers, hair accessories)

- Social/home activities (like renting videos, extended bedtime, use of television/computer)
- Parental praise/self-praise

To build momentum, we suggest starting out with a few small, tangible items. As your child progresses through the exposures, rewards should include more social/home activities. Rewards should be given after the successful completion of the exposures, which means after your child makes it through an exposure. Anxiety is both expected and allowed. Be sure to give your child plenty of praise to reward his efforts.

Once your child successfully completes an exposure, he is expected to handle a similar situation without a reward. Subsequent rewards are reserved for completing more challenging situations from his separation-fears list (chapter 4).

The final phase of the rewards system is to help your child learn to use self-praise (like "I'm proud of myself"). Overcoming separation anxiety is the best reward. In chapters 6 and 7, we'll show you how to effectively implement rewards using our real-life stories.

Summary

In this chapter, we helped you empower your child with cognitive therapy techniques and relaxation-based coping skills. We also presented a plan for keeping your child motivated as he confronts separation-related situations.

Now it's time to put it all together and help your child overcome his separation anxiety. In chapter 6, we'll use our real-life stories to show you how to help your child be alone and/or sleep alone.

Chapter 6

Managing Fear of Being and Sleeping Alone

Lenore slept through the night. I never thought it would happen.

—Kate

CHAPTER OBJECTIVES

In this chapter you will learn:

- Step-by-step plans for managing your child's fear of being alone
- Step-by-step plans for managing your child's fear of sleeping alone
- How to help your child overcome resistance to experiencing separation anxiety

ARE YOU READY?

It's time to put it all together to help your child overcome her separation fears. As you prepare, remember that every child progresses at her own pace. For this reason, build your child's confidence by initially helping her take small steps. Take a deep breath. Think in healthy ways. We'll guide you every step of the way. Let's begin with Debbie's step-by-step exposure plan for managing a fear of being alone.

DEBBIE: ALONE DURING THE DAY

As you know, Debbie is seven years old and follows her mom, Janice, around the house. She refuses to spend time in her room alone without the promise of Janice being nearby and checking on her every few minutes. In addition, she tags along as Janice does the laundry, throws out the garbage, talks on the phone, or goes to the bathroom. Debbie is afraid of becoming sick and needs Janice to be her medical monitor. Janice wants Debbie to feel more secure and to learn how to handle being alone. Janice wants her life back.

In order to accomplish this, Debbie needs to be exposed to being alone in her house during the day. Therefore, Janice will be working with her to stay alone first in her room for a brief time, then for longer, then finally in other locations in their house.

Next, we'll guide you to structure the beginning exposures for your child who is afraid to be alone in the house during the day. If your child's separation anxiety is expressed differently, please continue to read through this section, since we will be explaining how to structure a gradual set of exposures. You will find specific exposures that are more applicable to your child as we continue to go through each of our real-life examples over the next few chapters. Let's get started.

Beginning Exposures

The goal is to have your child become used to being alone in her home during the day. For your first exposure, have her sit in her room alone for one minute, while you stand in the hallway outside the door. Try this a few times, perhaps over the course of a few days. Your next step is to extend the *duration* of your child's exposure, then the *distance* you are from her. When she feels fairly comfortable with her first exposure, extend it to five minutes with you standing in the hallway. Next, try five minutes with you around the corner, out of her sight. This last exposure may be particularly difficult, as your child won't be able to look at you for reassurance. To help ease her anxiety, try any and all of the following:

- Reassure your child that you're in the hallway ("I'm still here").
- Agree to check on your child once or twice.
- Use distractors (reading a book, coloring, playing games) to help keep your child preoccupied.

THE ROLE OF DISTRACTION

Without a doubt, allowing your child to be distracted will help with challenging exposures. The problem, however, is that distraction only temporarily lessens your child's anxiety simply because she is preoccupied. Distraction is another form of avoidance because it takes away your child's chance to feel the fear which is needed for her to overcome her anxiety. Thus, we recommend that you allow your child to use distraction only as a first step in getting through difficult exposures.

SETTING REALISTIC GOALS

We recommend that you continue this sequence until your child can comfortably stay alone in her room for thirty minutes during the day. The idea is to gradually lengthen the duration of the exposures while you reduce and ultimately eliminate her safety signals. Of course, if your child is like Debbie (strong willed), she will need some help in the form of coping tools and possible rewards to achieve this goal.

For example, Janice encouraged Debbie to practice the relaxation exercises ("take a deep breath," "do the stomach exercise," "show me the fists"), offered to check on her briefly two times (if needed), and promised small trinkets for each exposure. Once accomplished, however, Janice expected Debbie to stay in her room for thirty minutes without a problem or a reward.

Midway

Now it's time to expose your child to similar situations but in different rooms of your house. Doing so will build your child's confidence and better prepare her for more challenging situations. For your first exposure, have her stay alone in the kitchen for one minute while you stand in the hallway outside the door. Try this a few times, perhaps over the course of a few days. Your next step is to extend the duration of your child's exposure, then the distance you are from her. When she feels fairly comfortable in the kitchen, extend it to five minutes with you standing in the hallway. Next, try five minutes with you around the corner, out of her sight. Once the kitchen exposure is successfully completed, you can set up a similar set of exposures for spending time in the living room. You can now include other exposures based on your child's specific fears (for instance, going to the bathroom or brushing teeth).

Once your child has completed these steps, you're ready to help her attempt some more demanding exposures. Up until now, all of the situations involved your child being on the same floor as family members. If your house has more than one level, you will now ask her to spend time on a different floor. If your house has only one level, you can try these exposures at a friend or relative's house or simply move onto the next section.

The first step is to ask your child to go upstairs and bring down an item of her choice while family members remain downstairs. If your child gives you a hard time, consider allowing her to run quickly up and down the stairs or having her walk while you remain at the bottom of the staircase. Once this exposure is accomplished, send your child upstairs to do something such as get dressed, brush her teeth, or use the bathroom.

Homestretch

This is what you've been waiting for. At this point, your child will have demonstrated an ability to stay alone in different rooms of your house as well as being on a different floor for short intervals. Now, it's time for your child to learn to cope while you're busy with activities. As a first step, attempt the following exposures on the same floor as your child. She can remain in her room or some other place as long as she cannot see you. Start out by planning exposures where you will go to the bathroom alone, talk on the phone privately, or any other similar activity.

Now, these situations may seem similar to some of the beginning and midway exposures. Thus, you may not expect much of an increase in your child's separation anxiety. Keep in mind, however, that previously, your child was moving away from you. Now, you are moving away from her, which may make her feel less secure and more anxious. For this reason, once again, consider any of the following to help your child initially get through the exposures:

- Reassure your child ("I'm still in the bathroom," "I'm still on the phone").
- Use distractors.
- Keep initial exposures short (one to two minutes).

Once your child is able to successfully complete these exposures, you can gradually increase the duration of time she is to be alone and slowly remove your reassurances and her use of distractors.

The next step, of course, is for you to engage in necessary activities on a different floor from your child without being followed, for example doing the laundry or throwing out the garbage. Again, your child may experience increased anxiety. If necessary, as a first step, consider any of the following to help your child get through the exposures:

- Allow your child to remain at the top of the stairs.
- Gradually change the time limit (one minute . . . five minutes . . . ten minutes).
- Use distractors.
- Reassure your child by saying, "I'm in the garage," or "I'm folding the laundry."

By now you should have completed the basic exposure plan for your child. The next step is for you to gradually increase the amount of time your child is away from you, extending it until your child can comfortably be away from you for thirty minutes or more. If your child's separation anxiety has been fully addressed, please feel free to skip ahead to chapter 10, where we'll help you evaluate your child's overall progress. Otherwise, up next is our step-by-step plan to help your child manage her fear of sleeping alone. We illustrate with our real-life story of Lenore and her mother, Kate.

LENORE: STAYING ALONE AT NIGHT

As you know, Lenore is ten years old and has been sleeping in her parents' bed for the past three months. Lenore is terrified that an intruder will break into the house. She panics at the slightest noise, such as the wind, the radiator, or a passing car. Lenore is afraid of being alone at night and needs her mother, Kate, to be her security guard. Kate wants Lenore to be able to sleep alone in her own room at night so they can both get a good night's rest.

In order to accomplish this, Lenore needs to be exposed to being alone in her room at night. Therefore, Kate will be working with her to stay alone in her room first after dinner, then later in the evening, and finally to sleep alone.

Now we'll guide you to structure the beginning exposures for your child who is afraid to sleep alone in her room. If your child's separation anxiety is expressed differently, please continue to read through this section, since you will gain more knowledge that you will be able to apply to your own child's exposure plan in the coming chapters. Let's get started.

Beginning Exposures

The goal here is to have your child initially become used to staying alone in her bedroom in the evening. For your first exposure, have her spend ten minutes alone in her bedroom after dinner. Most children who fear sleeping alone will not resist this preliminary step. Unlike Debbie, who is afraid to be alone at any time of the day, Lenore is most afraid at bedtime. Of course, she will start to worry once it becomes dark outside. For this reason, help your child feel secure by letting her decide how far away you will be from her bedroom. For example, you could be in the hallway, bathroom, or kitchen. Try this a few times, if necessary.

Your next step is to extend the duration of your child's exposure, then the distance you are from her, and finally, the timing of the exposure. When she feels comfortable with the first exposure, extend it to thirty minutes. Next, try ten minutes with you around the corner, out of her sight. Try this a few times, increasing the duration up to thirty minutes. Now you're ready to change the timing of the exposure by having her stay alone in her bedroom for thirty minutes before bedtime.

Clearly, the last situation will be the most difficult for your child since it is so close to her bedtime. If your child gives you a hard time with this exposure, consider trying any of the following:

- Agree to check on your child once or twice.
- Use distractors.
- Reassure your child that you will still stay with her at night for now.

SETTING REALISTIC GOALS

We recommend that you continue this sequence of exposures until your child can comfortably stay alone in her bedroom for thirty minutes before bedtime. To accomplish this goal, Kate encouraged Lenore to ask herself evidence-based questions (like, "What's the most likely thing that could happen?" "What's the best thing that could happen?"), to use coping thoughts ("I can stay alone"), and to praise herself for her efforts ("Good job," "I'm proud of myself"). In addition, Lenore received greater access to computer activities for completing exposures.

Midway

Now it's time to get your child to sleep in her own bed. As a first step, you can agree to stay with your child in her bedroom for the entire night. In exchange for agreeing to stay for the night, be sure to minimize physical contact with her following the nighttime routine. For example, you can sit in a comfortable chair in her bedroom. Once your child starts to fall asleep within thirty minutes of being in her own room, you'll be ready to attempt the next step.

This next step is staying with your child until she falls asleep and then returning to your bedroom. Naturally, this step is more difficult and may present a major challenge. Some children may feel secure knowing that the parent will stay until they fall asleep. Other children, however, may be unable to rest knowing the parent will not be on call. For example, if your child is a worrier like Lenore, she may remain awake for several hours. This is where your parenting style comes into play.

For example, the protector, who doesn't want to cause her child any distress, may agree to stay the night. The evaluator, who thinks her child should be able to sleep alone by now, may become frustrated and leave her child's room prematurely. The negotiator may set some limits, but due to her own fatigue may end up staying for the night.

If your child is now having trouble falling asleep, there are a few intermediate steps you can take. For example, you can stay with your child until she falls asleep and then remain in the hallway for the rest of the night with a pillow and blanket. Once your child is comfortable with this arrangement, you can stay with your child until she falls asleep, and then return to your bedroom, leaving the pillow or blanket in the hallway.

The last situation, of course, may be the most difficult for your child. However, as long as one of your personal items remains in the hallway, your child may still feel that you're readily available, and be less likely to seek your attention.

To minimize sleep deprivation, for both you and your child, consider attempting these steps over the weekend. For example, encourage your child to stay up as late as possible. By doing so, she may be too tired to worry and will be more likely to sleep through the night. Once your child accomplishes this goal without you in her bedroom, you will be much closer to getting a good night's rest. We recommend that your child sleep through the night on at least two occasions before proceeding to the next step.

Homestretch

This is what you've been waiting for. At this point, your child will have demonstrated the ability to sleep alone in her room, once she falls asleep. Now it's time for your child to learn to fall asleep on her own, without you present. You will now stay with your child during the nighttime routine but leave before she falls asleep.

The fact that your child has slept through the night a handful of times is a tribute to you. She is likely beginning to feel safer at night and not nearly as worried about an intruder. Nevertheless, your child may still have difficulty falling asleep on her own, especially if she hasn't attempted to do so in a long time.

The idea is to have your child remain in her bedroom when you say good night or in the event of a night waking. In our experience, children with more passive temperaments like Lenore will be obedient but may call you repeatedly, go to the bathroom, or simply make excuses so you will visit. Children with more intense temperaments may not let you leave their rooms or may visit you throughout the night. If your child gives you a difficult time, we recommend any of the following:

- Stay in your bedroom (door open) and encourage your child to practice coping skills.
- Help your child stay alone with distractors.

- Use a baby monitor.
- Use walkie-talkies.

In our experience, the use of a baby monitor or a walkie-talkie can make all the difference in helping a child negotiate her fear of sleeping alone. For example, a baby monitor helped satisfy Lenore's security-guard needs. She felt safe that Kate was on call for any suspicious noises coming from her bedroom, and as a result, she was able to sleep through the night.

Sometimes, however, one-way communication is not enough. If your child repeatedly visits you at night, we recommend using walkie-talkies. That way your child can talk to you while still staying in her room. Keep the communication brief and encourage your child to practice her coping exercises. Over time, you can gradually limit how many times your child can call you and eventually simply allow her one emergency communication.

Finally, one last strategy for younger children is to reward your child for sleeping through the night a certain number of times by having a planned sleepover with you one weekend. Now, staying with you is the result of your child's coping efforts rather than separation anxiety and can be an event the entire family can look forward to and enjoy.

Summary

In this chapter, we guided you through our step-by-step plans for helping your child manage her fear of being alone and/or sleeping alone. In chapter 7, we'll show you how to help your child manage her abandonment fears with our real-life stories of Peter, Mark, and their families.

Chapter 7

Managing Fear of Being Abandoned

Mark is like a different child. He actually looks forward to playdates.

—Peggy

CHAPTER OBJECTIVES

In this chapter you will learn:

- Step-by-step plans for managing your child's fear of getting sick
- Step-by-step plans for managing your child's fear of being abandoned
- How to help your child overcome resistance to experiencing separation anxiety

EATING WITHOUT FEAR

As you know, children with separation anxiety often experience unpleasant feelings in their bodies. This usually occurs when they know they will need to separate from a safe person. They are also more likely to connect these feelings to potential unpleasant outcomes (like vomiting, choking, or becoming physically ill). If there is even a shred of evidence that your child could become ill, he may refuse to eat before or during separations or to attend events at all. For this reason, we begin with helping your child eat at home and other places, then address social and extracurricular activities. Let's take a look at Peter's step-by-step exposure plan.

PETER: EATING BEFORE ACTIVITIES

As you know, Peter is fourteen years old and rarely leaves his house other than to attend school or play on the baseball team. Every morning he feels nauseous before school and does not eat breakfast or lunch. He is afraid of becoming sick and needs an adult to be his lifeguard. At school, Peter visits the nurse often and avoids eating in order to minimize his anxiety. Peter's parents, Rick and Mary, would like their son to feel secure enough to be able to eat breakfast and lunch without a fear of becoming sick and not having someone to rescue him.

In order to accomplish this, Peter needs to be exposed to eating something—first at home for breakfast, then lunch at school, and finally, to be able to eat in less familiar settings.

Next, we'll guide you to structure the beginning exposures for your child who is afraid to eat due to a fear of becoming sick. If your child's separation anxiety is expressed differently, please continue to read through this section, since you will gain more knowledge that you will be able to apply to your own child's exposure plan in the coming chapters.

Beginning Exposures

The goal is for your child to be able to eat breakfast. To help Peter feel more in charge, Mary and Rick let him decide what to eat (half a bagel). Anything Peter chose would have been okay. The important thing is that your child goes to school thinking or feeling that becoming ill is a possibility. This exposure will help your child realize that he can eat something without becoming physically ill. Of course, for your child to do this, like Peter, he may spend some time in the nurse's office. If your child is eating very small amounts of food, repeat this exposure by having him gradually increase the amount of food he is eating.

Your next step is to make your child's exposures more challenging by reducing his reliance on safety signals. First, change the duration of time that he uses the safety signals. In Peter's case the amount of time that he was allowed to spend in the nurse's office was cut in half. Once that is successful, you can change your child's access to safe persons. For example, if your child visits the nurse in the morning and afternoon, have him skip the morning visit. Finally, change your child's access to safe objects, if any. At this point, Peter was instructed to keep his water bottle in his locker in the morning.

Limiting your child's access to safe persons and objects may be difficult. For this reason, Mary and Rick allowed Peter access to the nurse and/or his water bottle in the afternoon. Simply knowing that he had access to the nurse and his water bottle later in the day helped Peter to feel more secure.

SETTING REALISTIC GOALS

At this point, your child should feel increasingly comfortable eating something for breakfast before attending school. The idea is to encourage (rather than pressure) your child to eat different things and work toward consuming a regular meal. Once accomplished, you can help your child eat something for lunch in the school cafeteria as well as at other people's houses.

Midway

Now it's time to get your child to eat in settings outside of the home. We'll begin with lunch at school. Many children often retreat to a safe person's (nurse, social worker, or guidance counselor) office during the lunch period. For this reason, you can build your child's confidence by helping him to spend time in the cafeteria. Your child's first step is to spend five minutes in the cafeteria without any expectation of eating. Repeat this exposure, gradually increasing the time, until your child is able to remain in the cafeteria for the entire lunch period. At this point, or if your child was already comfortable in the cafeteria, you're ready to begin exposing him to actually eating in the cafeteria. Initially pack comfort foods and gradually work toward having him eat a regular meal.

You can follow a similar sequence for helping your child eat at a close friend's or relative's house. Since children who fear becoming ill rarely look forward to family outings involving eating, be sure to reward their efforts with a pleasant activity-based reward. Again, as a first step, eating is not required. Once your child feels comfortable in these settings, you can consider varying his access to safe persons and objects and the duration or length of the exposure, as during the school-based exposures.

Once your child is able to eat at a familiar friend or relative's house, you're ready to attempt some more demanding exposures. As a first step, have your child eat something at a less familiar home of a friend or extended family member. Have your child attend and eat at social events such as a movie or extracurricular activity at school. Continue this sequence of exposures, varying access to safety signals and duration until your child can comfortably attend occasions at a few unfamiliar homes and social events with family members. You can also vary the distance from home or closeness to a bathroom, to make the exposures more challenging.

Homestretch

Up until now, all of the exposure situations have involved family members. The real challenge, of course, is to send your child out into the world without his lifeguard. You can follow a similar sequence of exposures as above, without your presence.

Naturally, your child will become more apprehensive since he will be accompanied by individuals who are perceived as less safe and less likely to be of help in the event physical illness should occur. For this reason, let your child decide what he needs during the exposures to still feel reasonably secure.

In Peter's case, he chose his water bottle and two phone calls, if needed, to his parents. With repeated exposures, however, Peter's confidence grew, and he eventually let go of both his water bottle and the need to call his parents.

Up next is our step-by-step plan to help your child manage his fear of being dropped off and/or not getting picked up from various places. We illustrate with our real-life story of Mark and his mother, Peggy.

MARK: BEING DROPPED OFF

As you remember, Mark is nine years old and refuses to go anywhere other than school unless his mother, Peggy, stays with him. He refuses to take the school bus to or from school, insisting that his mother drive him in both directions. In addition, Mark insists that his mother stay home while he is in school so he won't have to worry about her. If Peggy goes out in the evening or on the weekend, Mark calls his mother repeatedly on her cell phone until she returns home. He feels the need to be his mother's parental bodyguard.

Many children with separation anxiety worry that bad things will happen to them or to primary caregivers during anticipated separations. This was certainly true for Mark. His constant awareness of Peggy's whereabouts repeatedly reassured him that nothing bad happened to his mother. But if Mark was unaware of his mother's whereabouts, even for a brief time, he would have assumed that something bad did happen. Thus, Peggy has to show Mark that he can separate and nothing bad will happen to either one of them.

In order to accomplish this, Mark needs to be exposed to being dropped off and staying without his mother at age-appropriate social and recreational activities. Therefore, Peggy will be working with him to first take the bus to and from school, then to attend familiar activities, and finally to attend less familiar activities without her presence.

Next, we'll guide you to structure the beginning exposures for your child who is afraid to be dropped off at activities and fears for your safety while he is away from you. If your child's primary issue is refusal to attend school, please continue to read through this section, since you will continue to gain knowledge that you will be able to apply to your own child's exposure plan. You will find more specific examples of children with school refusal in the next two chapters. Let's take a look at Mark's step-by-step exposure plan.

Beginning Exposures

The goal is to help your child take the bus to and from school. So, start by having your child take the bus home from school. To help him feel more secure, Peggy agreed to follow Mark's bus home from school. In our experience, most children are willing to take the bus home. It's going to school that tends to be a problem. If your child is already taking the bus home, help him take the bus to school. As long as your child willingly takes the bus, initially do whatever he needs to feel safe.

Once your child is comfortably taking the bus home from school, it's time to make the exposures more challenging by changing first his access to safe people. For example, tell your child that you won't follow the bus from school to home, but that you will stay home during the bus trip and be there to meet the bus.

Now it's time to change the timing of events by having your child take the bus to school with you following the bus in your car. Once your child is comfortable with this situation, have him take the bus to school without you following the bus. Both of these situations will be difficult for your child, since you are slowly removing his safety signals.

SETTING REALISTIC GOALS

At this point, your child should feel increasingly comfortable taking the bus to or from school. He is learning that separations don't necessarily result in dreaded outcomes.

For some children, however, taking the bus to or from school is quite an ordeal. If this is true for your child, a realistic goal for him may be taking the bus to or from school once or twice a week. You can also follow a similar sequence of exposures if your child has difficulty taking the bus to or from camp.

Midway

Now it's time to expose your child to other situations that he is avoiding, such as playdates or social/extracurricular events like sports practices. However, some children, like Mark, may not have attended any of these situations for many months. Mark was even starting to refuse to have friends come over to his house. He was already anticipating having to reciprocate the playdate by going to a friend's house. If your child is having a hard time here, we recommend the following sequence of exposures as a first step.

Plan a few playdates for your child at your home. When your child is comfortable with playdates at home, plan a playdate at a friend's house he has been to before, while you stay the entire time. Continue to plan similar playdates without the expectation of being dropped off, for now. Finally, have your child attend a birthday party or extracurricular activity while you stay the entire time. If your child has been refusing to attend events, even if you promise to stay, consider connecting his attempt to small tangible or activity-based rewards. Once your child completes these exposures, he will have the confidence to attempt more demanding exposures.

Now you're ready to repeat the above exposures while gradually removing yourself from the situation. First, vary duration by first having your child stay alone at the event for five minutes, then ten minutes, and so forth. Next, you can vary distance. First stay in the same building, then in the same shopping center, then another location nearby. You can also vary your child's access to safe actions and objects. Feel free initially to allow your child to have a safe object with him, while you are not present. If necessary, allow your child to call you first three times, then twice, then only once, if needed.

Be sure to help your child make the connection that he is attending these situations without you, even if it's just for a few minutes, rather than emphasizing how much help he needed. Encourage your child to use the evidence from the previous exposures to develop coping thoughts, for example, "I can stay at the party for fifteen minutes and nothing bad happens." Once your child has mastered these exposures, gradually reduce his reliance on safety signals by planning exposures without them. Be prepared to use small rewards, as needed, for your child's ability to conquer those situations on his own.

Once your child is regularly attending social situations, you're ready to help him manage the next step. But remember, some children may continue to need five to ten minutes of warm-up time before being ready for a parent to leave.

Homestretch

Now it's time to help your child attend playdates and other social and extracurricular activities that may make him feel less secure, such as going to a new friend's house. You can follow a similar sequence of exposures as outlined above. Initially, do whatever it takes to help your child feel secure, even if you need to stay for the entire time. As your child feels increasingly comfortable attending these situations, you can then gradually remove yourself as before.

Depending upon your success with these exposures, use your judgment in deciding whether your child should attempt a sleepover at this time. If your child is like Mark, he will be very reluctant to sleep over at anyone's house. For this reason, we recommend a series of smaller steps.

First plan an evening playdate for your child without any expectation of sleeping over. Next, have your child sleep over at a close relative's house while you stay the entire time. Finally, have your child sleep over at a close relative's house without you.

Since thinking about the sleepover is often more difficult than actually sleeping over, setting up the potential sleepover as an evening playdate often works well. Of course, it may take a few attempts before your child stays for the entire night. For this reason, emphasize your child's efforts rather than how long he stays. Being able to sleep over at a friend's house will certainly boost your child's confidence. But remember, as long as your child regularly separates from you, the sleepover can wait. You may want to focus your energies on helping your child manage the final step.

Up until now, all of the situations involved Mark separating from Peggy. When Mark was dropped off at places like school, a friend's house, or a party, the activities at hand helped to distract him. Now, however, Peggy is leaving Mark at home with less safe individuals such as other family members or a babysitter. Distraction is no longer very helpful since Mark feels considerably less secure.

For these reasons, your child may strongly resist your leaving him at home with other family members or a babysitter. If your child gives you a hard time here, as a first step, agree to call him when you arrive at your destination and when you leave to come home. In addition, help your child practice the cognitive and/or relaxation exercises before you leave and after you come home. Help your child understand the legitimate reasons for your possible lateness in arriving home, as illustrated in chapter 5.

More importantly, on occasion, arrive a few minutes late in coming home or picking him up from school, a friend's house, or other activity. Once your child recognizes that you can be late without negative consequences, his fear will diminish.

In addition to varying the duration, distance from home, and access to safe persons and actions, you can also eventually vary the planning of the exposures by first giving advance notice, and then unexpectedly leaving the house.

For example, suddenly announcing that you have to do a quick food shop will be more challenging for your child than a planned get-together with friends. In addition, over time, we recommend that you become increasingly nonspecific regarding your whereabouts. For example, rather than promising that you will stay home for the entire day while your child is at school, you can say, "I'll stay nearby." You can continue to challenge your child as long as you take steps to help him to feel reasonably secure.

Summary

In this chapter, we guided you through our step-by-step plans for helping your child manage his separation-related abandonment fears. In chapter 8, we'll explain how your child's separation anxiety can lead to school refusal. Using four additional real-life stories as examples, we'll help you develop specific action plans so that your child or adolescent can effectively confront the different types of school refusal. If your child is not refusing to attend school, you can skip ahead to chapter 10, where we'll help you evaluate your child's overall progress.

Chapter 8

When Your Child Refuses to Go to School

[Looking pale, holding his stomach] *I can't go to school!*

—Dan

Mommy don't go! [clinging to Rachel]

—Becky

CHAPTER OBJECTIVES

In this chapter you will learn:

- How to develop school-refusal lists (exposures) for each type of school refusal
- How to plan and structure your child or adolescent's exposures
- How to use our safety-signal selector

THE NATURE OF SCHOOL REFUSAL

School refusal occurs in many forms and often involves different degrees of anxiety, avoidance, and/or absences. At its simplest level, a child may resist getting ready in the morning but will ultimately attend school without further distress. At its most severe, a child or adolescent may refuse to attend school at all and have a long-standing pattern of absenteeism.

As many as 75 percent of children with separation anxiety experience some form of school-refusal behavior. However, the majority of these children successfully adjust to school. For example, Peter (misfortune teller) had features of school-refusal behavior. He felt physically sick each morning, often skipped breakfast, and stayed nearby safe people (nurse, coach, best friend) throughout the school day.

This chapter is about school refusal that significantly interferes with a child or adolescent's ability to *go to* and/or *stay in* school. When this occurs, school refusal may be the result of a broad range of anxiety-related concerns (like social anxiety, worry, panic, separation anxiety) and/or depression. In our experience, children and adolescents with these concerns typically struggle to:

- Get ready in the morning

- Enter the school building
- Stay in school without parental support
- Attend school due to social anxiety/panic/depression

Your child may experience one of these problems in isolation or have features of more than one of these types of school refusal. For purposes of illustration, we'll take you through each type separately. We recommend that you carefully review the entire chapter and then focus on the sections most relevant for helping your child or adolescent. First, we address when a child resists getting ready in the morning.

MORNING PREPARATION

Difficulty getting ready in the morning is often about the anticipation of going to school. Once this transition is managed, most children cope adequately during the school day. Let's address how to help your child if she resists getting ready in the morning.

Eggshells for Breakfast

Are you walking on eggshells? Has the morning routine become completely unbearable? If so, which of the following behaviors does your child exhibit?

- Refuses to get out of bed/leave room
- Resists dressing self
- Refuses to pack backpack
- Insists on only favorite foods for breakfast
- Throws temper tantrums
- Refuses to take the school bus

WHY IS THIS HAPPENING?

Are you a morning person or a night owl? If you feel best in the morning, it may be harder to understand why your child struggles to get ready in the morning. Most children that have difficulty getting ready in the morning also have difficulty getting ready to go to sleep at night. At its simplest level, your child's temperament may require more transition time during the morning and evening routines.

Of course, a second and more important factor is your child's anxiety about going to school. Her anxiety is likely to be expressed in the form of a strong fear of getting sick. Your child may be completely convinced that she is physically ill and will therefore demand to stay home from school. She may complain of aches and pains, fever, fatigue, and may move in a sluggish fashion. This is especially true for younger children. For example, unlike Peter, a younger child may have a lesser ability to understand the true reality of her physical feelings. In other words, to feel sick is to *be* sick.

Finally, if your child is strong willed, any variation from her expected routine or the suggestion that her physical feelings are anxiety related may result in an explosive outburst. You will either be walking on eggshells or engaged in constant power struggles to get your child to go to school. We illustrate with our real-life story of Jack and his parents, Susan and Jim.

Jack's Example

Susan and Jim describe their eight-year-old son, Jack, as sensitive, intense, and strong willed. He is prone to temper outbursts when things don't go his way. Jack is overly critical of his actions and has few friends.

In the morning, Jack refuses to get out of bed. He insists that he feels sick and needs to stay home. If Susan suggests that he is nervous about going to school, Jack becomes enraged and shouts, "I hate you." At that point, Jim usually intervenes and a shouting match ensues.

By the time Jack is ready for breakfast, he is twenty minutes behind schedule. If he feels capable of eating any breakfast, it must be French toast. He insists on having a peanut-butter sandwich (without jelly on white bread with the crusts removed) for lunch. If Susan suggests that he eat something else, Jack accuses her of not loving him.

Jack refuses to take the school bus in the morning. He won't willingly leave the house unless Jim drives him in his car. Once at school, Jack typically has a good day—but rarely admits so.

VIEWING YOUR CHILD'S MORNING DISTRESS

If your child's behavior resembles Jack's, do you view her morning distress as manipulative? We certainly understand why you would do so. Unlike Mark, who fears for his mother's safety, and Peter, who fears throwing up, Jack does not appear overly concerned about his mother or himself. Rather, he seems to be using his physical feelings and antics as a means of getting what he wants in the morning (sleeping late, his choice of breakfast/lunch, a ride to school). And while there may be some truth to this view, thinking this way will undoubtedly result in intense power struggles.

Remember, every child experiences anxiety in her unique way. Jack is indeed anxious about going to school. The process of getting ready for school represents a difficult transition. Younger children are more likely to experience the distress of this transition in the form of physical feelings. The physical feelings are genuine and tell the child that she cannot cope. The child may adhere to a rigid morning routine in order to feel more secure.

There is hope, however, for a more peaceful morning routine. We'll show you how to accomplish this goal with your child using our step-by-step plans in chapter 9. But first, let's take a look at the school-refusal list that could serve as possible exposures for Jack.

JACK'S SCHOOL-REFUSAL LIST

Previously, we presented lists for each child's separation fears. Now, we do the same for each school-refusal case. The school-refusal lists will include all of the situations that the child has difficulty confronting or completely avoids. Overcoming school refusal, like separation fears, also requires confronting challenging situations. We'll ask you to prepare a similar school-refusal list for your child based on your family's experiences. Once that is complete, we'll provide a list of safety-signal needs for the same real-life example. Again, safety signals are those people, places, objects, or actions that make one feel less scared in an anxiety-provoking situation. Then, we'll ask you to provide a similar list of safety needs for your child. You will be able to make your child's initial exposures less anxiety-provoking and later exposures more challenging by referring to the safety-signal selector. Be sure to review each type of school refusal since many children exhibit features of more than one type. This way, the school-refusal list that you eventually construct will be as accurate as possible. Let's take a look at the school-refusal list that could serve as possible exposures for Jack.

GETTING READY FOR SCHOOL ON TIME:

- Awakens with minimal parental prompts
- Awakens to own alarm clock
- Gets dressed/brushes teeth/organizes school materials with minimal prompts
- Eats something for breakfast

DEVELOPING FLEXIBILITY WITH MORNING ROUTINE:

- Eats something different for breakfast (several days)
- Takes the bus to school (periodically)
- Organizes school materials the night before
- Maintains a good attitude without complaints or outbursts

The idea is to help your child gradually become more independent, flexible, and responsible for managing her morning routine. While protecting your child's sense of security, you can take steps to help her become more flexible as well. A child like Jack is not necessarily afraid of going to school. Rather, it is the effort required to get ready that bothers him, especially if it varies from his regular routine. For this reason, resistance to getting ready in the morning usually takes the form of both anxiety (like a fear of getting sick) and agitation (resenting having to get ready). Please take a moment to list your child's school-refusal behaviors if she is giving you a difficult time getting ready for school.

YOUR CHILD'S SCHOOL-REFUSAL LIST (DIFFICULT MORNING ROUTINE)

SITUATIONS:

1: ____

2: ____

3: ____

4: ____

5: ____

Now, let's take a look at Jack's safety needs and safety signals.

JACK'S SAFETY NEEDS

Safe Persons: Susan and Jim

Safe Actions: Adhering to a rigid morning routine

Safe Places: Jim's car

As you can see, Jack does not have extensive safety needs. As long as Susan and Jim walk on eggshells and never deviate from his idea of a morning routine, Jack will not experience any distress. Of course, he may not get ready on time either. Please take a moment to list your child's safety needs if she is giving you a difficult time getting ready in the morning.

Safe Persons: ______________________________

Safe Objects: ______________________________

Safe Actions: ______________________________

Safe Places: ______________________________

SAFETY-SIGNAL SELECTION

Let's take another look at our safety-signal selector (figure 8.1) to determine how to make Jack's exposures gradually more challenging. As you remember, the safety-signal selector shows you the different dimensions of safety signals that can be varied to make exposures more or less challenging.

Safety-Signal Selector

ACCESS to safety signals

person	place	object	action

DURATION of exposure

under 5 minutes	up to 30 minutes	no time limit

DISTANCE from home, place, or person

within sight	within sound	neither

FAMILIARITY of situation, place, or person

familiar	unfamiliar

PLANNING of exposure

well in advance	short notice	unexpected

TIMING of exposure

day	night

Figure 8.1: Safety-Signal Selector

We can make Jack's exposures more challenging by varying his *access* to safe persons. For example, Susan and Jim can gradually limit their involvement in helping Jack to get ready in the morning. More importantly, we can vary the *familiarity* of Jack's morning routine by mixing up his rigid way of doing things. We'll show you how to accomplish these goals with your child using our step-by-step plans in chapter 9.

ENTERING THE SCHOOL BUILDING

For some children and adolescents, getting ready for school is not a big deal. Entering the school building, however, may provoke a full-blown panic.

A Time to Panic

Does your child appear to panic at the thought of entering the school building? If so, which of the following behaviors does she exhibit?

- Refuses to get out of your car (school parking lot)
- Clings to you outside the school building
- Cries, tantrums, becomes verbally and/or physically aggressive
- Refuses to get in line to enter school building
- Refuses to walk toward entrance door alone
- Refuses to enter the school building alone
- Refuses to walk to classroom alone

WHY IS THIS HAPPENING?

Like getting ready for school in the morning, the process of entering the school building is also a difficult transition for some children to negotiate. If your child panics in this situation, several factors may be involved.

First, your child is likely to be a worrier. Worriers tend to do their best to avoid thinking about unpleasant situations. Such a strategy is not ideal since it allows one's anxiety to build up. This is why it's so important to help your child identify, tolerate, and change her automatic thoughts (see chapter 5).

Second, your child may also have a passive personality. This means that she will only ask for your help when she is most anxious. For this reason, it may be hard to understand why your child is having so much difficulty entering the school building. After all, she copes well during the school day. Think of Lenore. Other than being fearful of sleeping alone at night, she appears to be well adjusted. Yet, Lenore is shy, sensitive, and a worrier.

Third, your child may not have a good sense of time. Situations may not seem real until they actually occur. If this is true, your child may suddenly become overwhelmed with panic as she tries to enter the school building. We illustrate with our real-life story of Dylan, and his mother, Roberta.

Dylan's Example

Roberta describes her nine-year-old son, Dylan, as shy, sweet, and sensitive. He worries about everything, and his feelings get hurt easily. Roberta explains that Dylan gets upset when other children misbehave or adults raise their voice. Dylan likes to play recreational sports but gets intimidated by competition and large groups. He does best when working or playing with others one to one. Dylan often gets overwhelmed and cries easily, especially in new situations.

Dylan looks forward to going to school each morning. He gets up, dresses, and eats his breakfast without a problem. The last two weeks, however, he has been refusing to get out of Roberta's car in the parking lot. If she insists that he do so, he cries, panics, and holds onto his seat. Thus, he has not attended school for the past two weeks.

THE SCHOOL'S ATTITUDE

If your child is like Dylan and has difficulty expressing emotions, school personnel may not be aware of the extent of her anxiety. As a result, they may view your child's behavior as oppositional (rather than based on anxiety) and insist that you separate from her prematurely. Doing so will likely result in explosive outbursts and further reinforce the notion that your child's behavior is indeed oppositional.

In Dylan's case, he started refusing to enter the school building well into the school year. What could have triggered such intense anxiety? Roberta later discovered that Dylan's teacher raised her voice regarding a general class matter. Dylan took this very personally and was afraid to enter the school building for fear of getting into trouble.

Like Roberta, you may need to educate school personnel about the importance of protecting your child's sense of security. In addition, if necessary, share with them our step-by-step plans to help ensure a smooth transition. Enlisting the support of the school psychologist or social worker can often be helpful in this process.

In chapter 9, we'll demonstrate Dylan's step-by-step plan for managing his fear of entering the school building. But first, let's take a look at the school-refusal list for Dylan that could serve as possible exposures.

DYLAN'S SCHOOL-REFUSAL LIST

Unlike Jack, who primarily has difficulty getting ready and going to school, Dylan's fear of entering school is more complex. His school refusal involves the parking lot, school building, and classroom.

SCHOOL PARKING LOT:

- Remains in car with parent
- Stays in parking lot but gets out of car (parent gets out as well)
- Walks toward school building (parent walks closely behind)

SCHOOL BUILDING:

- Walks with parent (no clinging) to the front door (after all students have entered)
- Quickly goes in and out of school building (after all students have settled in class)
- Enters the school building alone (parent stays on other side of door) then walks out

SCHOOL CLASSROOM:

- Walks with parent to class (parent remains in hallway until settled)
- Enters the school building with parent, school personnel walks to class (parent remains in hallway until settled)
- Enters the school building alone, school personnel walks to class (parent remains outside school door)

- Enters the school building with friend (parent remains in the parking lot until settled)
- Enters the school building alone or with friend (parent leaves the school grounds)

The idea is to break down the exposures into as many manageable situations for your child as you can. Dylan's school-refusal list, at first glance, may appear overwhelming. However, your child may not need as many steps. In fact, as long as you help your child maintain her sense of security, she may make rapid progress after the first few steps. Be sure to help your child manage her school refusal one stage at a time (leaving the parking lot, entering the school building). Please take a moment to list your child's school-refusal fears if she has difficulty entering the school building.

YOUR CHILD'S SCHOOL-REFUSAL LIST (ENTERING SCHOOL)

SITUATIONS:

1: ____________________

2: ____________________

3: ____________________

4: ____________________

5: ____________________

Now, let's take a look at Dylan's safety needs and safety signals.

DYLAN'S SAFETY NEEDS

Safe Persons: Roberta, best friend, teacher, school social worker

Safe Actions: Staying near Roberta, eliciting parental promises (stay in parking lot)

Safe Places: Roberta's car

As you can see, Dylan's safety needs are not as extensive as Peter's or Lenore's. This is because he is neither afraid of becoming sick nor afraid for his mother's personal safety. His safety signals will help him enter the school building and get settled in his classroom. If your child has features of separation anxiety (for instance, misfortune teller and/or timekeeper) as well as this type of school refusal, be sure to address all of her relevant safety needs. Please take a moment to list your child's safety needs if she has difficulty entering the school building.

Safe Persons: ____________________

Safe Objects: ____________________

Safe Actions: ____________________

Safe Places: ____________________

SAFETY-SIGNAL SELECTION

Let's take another look at our safety-signal selector to determine how to make Dylan's exposures gradually more challenging.

We can initially shorten the *duration* of time that he spends in the parking lot. For example, at first Dylan may refuse to get out of the car. As he becomes more comfortable, he will spend less time in the car and begin walking toward the school building. The second step is to vary the *distance* of his safe person

(Roberta) as he walks toward the school building and enters. The third and most important step is to vary his *access* to other relatively safe persons (best friend, teacher) as he finds his way to the classroom and settles down. We'll show you how to help your child accomplish these goals with our step-by-step plans in chapter 9.

REFUSING TO STAY IN SCHOOL (WITHOUT PARENTS)

In our experience, difficulty staying in school without a parent present is most characteristic of young children (three to five). The separation-related school refusal is about their first experience in a structured school setting (preschool/kindergarten).

Mommy, Don't Go!

If your child refuses to stay in school unless you remain with her for the entire time, which behaviors does she exhibit?

- Refuses to enter the classroom
- Clutches onto you for dear life
- Cries, tantrums
- Insists on sitting in your lap (in classroom)
- Refuses to participate in activities
- Refuses to eat lunch
- Refuses to use bathroom
- Stays by herself (if you leave the classroom)

WHY IS THIS HAPPENING?

For some children, managing preschool or kindergarten is a major life transition. If this is true for your child, several factors may be involved. For example, given your child's young age, she may have minimal experience separating from you. In addition, your child may not have yet developed secure attachments to individuals other than you or your partner/spouse. This means that at least initially, your child's refusal to separate may be due to the lack of perceived safe persons in the school setting. Your child (like most young children) may also have a poor sense of time. Thus, even during brief separations, she may feel like you will never return.

In addition to age-related separation factors, your child is probably emotionally sensitive (like the kids in all of our real-life stories) and has difficulty adjusting to unfamiliar or unexpected situations. If your child is strong willed and has an intense temperament, her resistance to staying in school may include a whole series of acting-out behaviors (crying, tantrums, clinging). Alternatively, if your child's temperament is more passive, she may separate from you but simply refuse to participate in activities. We illustrate with our real-life story of Becky and her parents, Rachel and David.

Becky's Example

Becky is a sweet and affectionate four-year-old girl. She has a contagious smile and a nervous laugh. Rachel and David explain that Becky is also strong willed and cries easily. Becky has trouble staying alone when other family members are present somewhere else in the house (see chapters 4 and 6). Also, Becky refuses to go on playdates or stay with a babysitter (see chapters 4 and 7).

Becky willingly enters her preschool classroom, but only if she can sit in Rachel's lap for the entire time. Becky also refuses to participate in classroom activities or play with the other children.

VIEWING YOUR CHILD'S REFUSAL TO SEPARATE

Do you view your child's school refusal as a nuisance? This is understandable, especially if you have to readjust your entire day so that you can stay with her at school. And while many children have trouble adjusting to preschool and/or kindergarten, this may be hardly comforting since your child's reactions may be more intense.

There is good news, however, regarding your child's early school-refusal behaviors. For instance, most preschools expect and are prepared to help children cope with separation-related school difficulties. In fact, some preschools include built-in transitions such as "Mommy and Me" to "All by Myself" programs. If your child is sensitive and you anticipate that she will have difficulty separating, take advantage of such a program before your child enters kindergarten.

Another benefit of your child's preschool jitters is that early intervention may help ensure a smoother school-related adjustment in the years to come. It's also easier to manage school refusal at this time than during elementary or middle school. The hardest part is that you may have to break down your child's exposures into smaller and more concrete steps given her young age and limited cognitive abilities. Let's take a look at Becky's school-refusal list to see what could serve as possible exposures.

BECKY'S SCHOOL-REFUSAL LIST

Dylan's school-refusal list is primarily about entering the school building and making it to class without experiencing panic. Once accomplished, the rest of his day typically goes smoothly. Becky's school refusal also involves entering the school building. However, Becky also needs time to become acclimated to the school grounds, her teacher, and the other children. In addition, her participation in school activities will also be a gradual process.

CREATING A COMFORT ZONE AT SCHOOL:

- Spends time on school grounds before or after school (parent present)
- Walks around empty classroom before or after school (parent present)
- Spends time with teacher before school (parent present)
- Spends time with teacher or another child in hallway before school (parent present)

ENHANCING THE COMFORT ZONE OUTSIDE OF SCHOOL:

- Plays with one or two children on school grounds after school (parent present)
- Plays with one or two children after school (parent's house)
- Plays with one or two children after school at friend's house (parent stays entire time)

PARTICIPATING IN SCHOOL ACTIVITIES:

- Joins circle time (sits on parent's lap)
- Joins circle time (parent stays nearby)
- Works on project/activity with teacher (parent stays nearby)

- Works on project/activity with teacher and one child (parent stays nearby)
- Plays with one child during free play (parent stays nearby)
- Works on project/activity with one child (teacher and parent stay nearby)

GRADUALLY REMOVING PARENT FROM THE CLASSROOM/SCHOOL BUILDING:

- Parent stays in classroom but at edge of the door
- Parent goes to bathroom (leaves child with safe object such as keys)
- Parent goes to car to get something (leaves child with safe object)
- Parent stays in hallway for a few minutes (visible)
- Parent stays in hallway (out of viewing distance for a few minutes)
- Parent walks around school grounds (five minutes)
- Parent sits in car in the parking lot (ten minutes)

As you can see, there are several levels in helping your child manage her fear of staying in school. Creating the comfort zone is designed to help your child warm up to the school environment. As long as you remain nearby, she will experience minimal anxiety. Of course, as the comfort zone extends to having playdates at other children's homes, your child's anxiety will incrementally rise. If you wish to address your child's abandonment fears outside the school setting, please follow our step-by-step plans for Mark in chapter 7.

Naturally, the real challenge will be to help your child first participate in school activities and ultimately cope as you gradually remove yourself from school. Of course, we realize this may be difficult if you work outside the home. It may be helpful to enlist the assistance of an extended family member (for instance, grandparent) or a trusted babysitter, if necessary.

Please take a moment to list your child's key school-refusal fears (school participation, parent phase out, etc.) if she has difficulty staying in preschool or kindergarten.

YOUR CHILD'S SCHOOL-REFUSAL LIST (STAYING IN PRESCHOOL)

SITUATIONS:

1: ____________________

2: ____________________

3: ____________________

4: ____________________

5: ____________________

Now, let's take a look at Becky's safety needs and safety signals.

BECKY'S SAFETY NEEDS

Safe Persons: Rachel and David

Safe Objects: Rachel's personal items (keys, wallet, handbag)

Safe Actions: Clinging to Rachel

Given her young age, Becky's safety signals are not yet fully developed. This means that only concrete objects/activities or visible safe persons will help her cope. Parental promises are too abstract and will provide her with little or no comfort. Rachel and David will work toward helping Becky feel safe in school and expanding her safe persons to include her teacher(s) and classmates. Please take a moment to list your child's safety needs if she has difficulty staying in preschool or kindergarten.

Safe Persons: ____

Safe Objects: ____

Safe Actions: ____

Safe Places: ____

SAFETY-SIGNAL SELECTION

Let's take another look at our safety-signal selector to determine how to make Becky's exposures gradually more challenging.

Once a comfort zone is created and Becky begins to feel safe at school, we can make Becky's exposures more challenging by initially changing the *distance* of her safe person (Rachel). For example, Rachel can move toward the door, step outside of the classroom briefly, and ultimately leave the school grounds. As Becky feels more secure participating in the classroom and integrating with her classmates, we can also gradually change the *duration* of time she separates from her mother. Most importantly, Becky needs to develop other safe persons in the classroom. We can do this by varying her *access* to teachers and friends. We'll show you how to accomplish these goals with your child using our step-by-step plans in chapter 9.

OLDER-CHILD SCHOOL REFUSAL

Some older children and adolescents may not be able to attend school at all. They may have extreme difficulty entering and staying in school, thereby accumulating an extensive record of absences.

I Can't Go to School

If entering and staying in school is a problem for your child or adolescent, which behaviors does she exhibit?

- Refuses to spend time on the school grounds
- Refuses to enter the school building
- Refuses to attend homeroom
- Refuses to attend academic classes
- Refuses to attend nonacademic classes (like gym)
- Refuses to do schoolwork at home
- Accrues a record of extensive absences

WHY IS THIS HAPPENING?

When adolescents refuse to attend and/or stay in school, it's usually not so much about separation anxiety (abandonment fears), but rather social anxiety, panic, or depression. Social anxiety is often the culprit and may be continued by both a fear of getting sick and/or worry about being embarrassed or humiliated. Adolescents that refuse school often have long-standing histories of school-refusal behavior. As a result, unlike children whose school refusal tends to be acute and short lived, school refusal in adolescents can be quite serious, chronic, and may result in extensive absences.

As with all of our real-life stories, temperament plays a role. If your adolescent's temperament is more passive, she may be more willing to cooperate in her efforts to attend and/or stay in school. However, unlike working with children, your adolescent's sheer physical size and strength of fearful beliefs may become major obstacles. We illustrate with our real-life story of Dan and his parents, Maggie and Kent.

Dan's Example

Dan is a timid and pleasant sixteen-year-old boy. He is an average student, loves sports, and has many friends. Dan is an avid member of his high-school basketball and baseball teams. During the last two weeks, however, Dan has refused to attend school. He gets ready for school but then freezes when it's time to leave. Looking pale, he holds his stomach and says, "I can't . . ."

His parents Maggie and Kent explain that Dan has always had sporadic school attendance. Absences usually coincided with peer issues, imminent tests, or athletic events. Despite being a top athlete, Dan constantly worries that he will make a mistake and is terrified of being embarrassed. Since missing school, Dan also refuses to go out in public (for instance, to a mall or restaurant) due to fear of being seen by his peers.

VIEWING YOUR ADOLESCENT'S SCHOOL REFUSAL

In most cases, schools tend to be fairly understanding of adolescent school refusal. This is especially true if there is any long-standing history of the problem and/or the adolescent is making some effort to attend/stay in school. The more important question is how do you view your adolescent's school refusal?

Do you find yourself saying or thinking things like, "I know she doesn't want to, but she *should* go to school. After all, she's fifteen or sixteen years old"? Adolescent school refusal can also be confusing when there is no evidence to support any adverse social consequences. But remember, when it comes to experiencing any kind of anxiety, simply thinking about situations is often far worse than actual outcomes.

In our experience, parents/guardians often have different views of their adolescent's school refusal. For example, Maggie was critical of Dan (the evaluator parenting style), and she felt his behavior was manipulative. She had trouble understanding how he could attend/stay in school some days and not even try on others. Kent, on the other hand, was more understanding (the protector parenting style) of Dan's school refusal and had difficulty setting limits with him. This was because Kent also struggled with social anxiety.

Differing parenting styles not only undermine each spouse/partner's efforts but also give the adolescent mixed messages. When given a choice, understandably so, most adolescents will side with the more protective parent. It's nothing personal. This is why it's so important for spouses/partners to be on the same wavelength and view their adolescent's school refusal in a healthy way (see chapter 3). Let's take a look at the school-refusal list that could serve as possible exposures for Dan.

DAN'S SCHOOL-REFUSAL LIST

- Spends time on school grounds (parking lot)
- Walks into the school building, then walks out (after everyone is in class)

- Spends time with guidance counselor or social worker
- Spends time in the library
- Spends lunch in the cafeteria (with friends)
- Attends homeroom
- Attends one nonacademic class
- Attends one academic class
- Stays in school until lunch (attends several classes)
- Goes to school for full day

Adolescent school refusal is rarely about insecure attachments and/or strong abandonment fears. Unlike Dylan and Becky, Dan does not want to be seen with his parents in school or social settings. In fact, he will be utterly embarrassed if he is seen with his parents. He does, however, see his dad as a source of support.

It's very important to get your adolescent to attend/stay in school in some capacity as soon as possible. Otherwise, your adolescent's continued avoidance may turn an acute situation into a chronic problem. Remember, spending time in the parking lot counts.

Please take a moment to list your adolescent's key school-refusal fears if she has difficulty entering and/or staying in high school.

YOUR ADOLESCENT'S SCHOOL-REFUSAL LIST (ENTERING/STAYING)

SITUATIONS:

1: ____

2: ____

3: ____

4: ____

5: ____

Now, let's take a look at Dan's safety needs and safety signals.

DAN'S SAFETY NEEDS

Safe Persons: Guidance counselor

Safe Actions: Calling Kent on cell phone

Safe Places: School library, bathroom, guidance office

Although Dan does not have separation anxiety, he still has safety needs that will help him enter and/or stay in school. His safe persons and places will help him stay in school while still staying out of sight so that he can avoid potential embarrassment. In addition, knowing that he can call his dad to pick him up helps him at least get to school. Unlike Peter, whose strong fear of getting sick necessitates the need to carry a water bottle, Dan's fear is more about the social consequences of becoming ill.

Please take a moment to list your adolescent's safety needs if she has difficulty entering and/or staying in school.

Safe Persons: ______________________________

Safe Objects: ______________________________

Safe Actions: ______________________________

Safe Places: ______________________________

SAFETY-SIGNAL SELECTION

Let's take one more look at our safety-signal selector to determine how to make Dan's exposures gradually more challenging.

The first step is to increase the *duration* of time that Dan spends on the school grounds. This means that he may spend a few days observing from the school parking lot. As he feels more comfortable and enters the school building, we can vary the *familiarity* of his places to stay. For example, at first Dan may be asked to spend time in the bathroom, library, or guidance office. In Dan's mind, these places are safe since there is a relatively low risk of being noticed and hence embarrassed.

As long as we help him maintain his sense of security, Dan can gradually spend time in homeroom, followed by nonacademic and then academic classes. Finally, we can vary his *access* to safe persons (moving from his dad via cell phone to the guidance counselor). We'll show you how to accomplish these goals with your adolescent using our step-by-step plans in chapter 9.

To help you keep track of the relationship between different types of school refusal and safety needs, please refer to the following table.

School-Refusal Types and Safety Needs

School-Refusal Type	**Safety Needs**	**Real-Life Story**
Refusal to Get Ready Sustained by a fear of getting sick, sensory issues, difficulty with transitions	*Rigid Morning Routine* Picky regarding clothes, food, and/or transportation	*Jack (8)* Parents: Susan and Jim
Refusal to Enter School Sustained by generalized worry and/or panic	*Safe Persons* Parent, best friend, teacher, social worker	*Dylan (9)* Parent: Roberta
Refusal to Stay in School (without parental support) Sustained by a fear of being abandoned	*Comfort Zone* Needs time to develop other safe persons	*Becky (4)* Parents: Rachel and David
Refusal to Attend School Sustained by social anxiety, panic, and/or depression	*Safe Places* Stay out of sight to avoid possible embarrassment (library, guidance office)	*Dan (16)* Parents: Maggie and Kent

Summary

In this chapter, we explained the relationship between separation anxiety and school refusal. In addition, we discussed the different types of school refusal and helped you develop school-refusal lists (exposures) and action plans for your child or adolescent. In chapter 9, using our real-life stories as examples, we'll show you how to help your child or adolescent manage school refusal with our step-by-step plans.

Chapter 9

Managing School Refusal

Jack went to school without a problem. He even ate cereal for breakfast!

—Susan

CHAPTER OBJECTIVES

In this chapter you will learn:

- Step-by-step plans for managing your child's fear of going to school
- Step-by-step plans for managing your child or adolescent's fear of staying in school
- How to help your child overcome resistance to going to and/or staying in school

ARE YOU READY?

It's time to put it all together and help your child or adolescent overcome his school refusal. We'll guide you every step of the way, from improving the morning routine to achieving full-time attendance. Let's begin with Jack's step-by-step plan for making the morning routine more pleasant.

JACK: MASTERING THE MORNING ROUTINE

As we indicated in the last chapter, Jack is eight years old and refuses to get out of bed in the morning. He insists that he feels sick and demands to stay home. If Susan or Jim suggests that he go to school, Jack throws a major temper tantrum. Everything is a power struggle, from getting ready in the morning to taking the school bus. And even when Jack cooperates, his needs are so particular. For instance, only eating French toast for breakfast or having a peanut-butter sandwich without jelly and the crusts removed for lunch. Susan and Jim simply want Jack to be more cooperative in the morning and learn how to be a bit more flexible in his ways of doing things.

In order to accomplish this, Susan and Jim need to make it worthwhile for Jack to get ready in the morning. By turning the morning routine into a game, getting out of bed, which has always been viewed as unpleasant, now is seen as an exciting challenge. Let's get started by helping your child play "The Race to Get Ready" (Drabman and Creedon 1979).

Beginning Exposures

First, figure out a realistic time that you would like to have your child ready for breakfast in the morning. Second, explain to your child that if he is ready for school and in the kitchen to eat breakfast before the time allotted, he will have won the race. Set the kitchen timer to help you keep track of the time. Third, help your child choose an appropriate reward for winning the race each morning. The reward should be given daily and include small, tangible items (like trading cards, stickers, or other playthings) or greater access to activities (television, computer, or staying up later at night).

Susan bought a pack of trading cards and offered Jack one card for each morning that he won the race. Another reward that works well is allowing your child to stay up an extra ten or fifteen minutes at night for each morning that he wins the race.

GENERAL GUIDELINES

- Prompt your child to get up in the morning a maximum of two times.
- Make a chart of morning responsibilities (get dressed, brush teeth, etc.) so that your child can check off each morning.

- Praise any effort on your child's part, even if he doesn't win a race.

- Help your child win (for instance, lay out clothes and/or organize school materials the night before).

Jack responded well to the game the first two weeks and won two packs of trading cards. Eventually, however, the trading cards lost their value, and Jack refused to get out of bed. For this reason, be sure to regularly vary rewards to sustain your child's motivation. In addition, play the game in non-school-related situations, like getting ready for church or temple. Doing so will help promote generalization of your child's "getting ready" skills. Over time, gradually phase out the rewards and praise your child's newfound sense of time management.

Midway

Once the excitement of winning the race wears off and your child thinks about eating breakfast, his physical anxiety will intensify. Initially, he may not be able to eat breakfast. This is why winning the race is about entering the kitchen on time rather than finishing breakfast. Your child may complain about feeling physically sick and demand to stay home. If he's as strong willed as Jack, don't argue about the true nature of his physical feelings (genuine sickness versus anxiety). Rather, use an objective indicator of sickness like a thermometer. It's hard to argue with a thermometer.

At this point, your child will likely relent and realize that he must go to school. However, he may still complain of feeling physically sick. Be sure to validate your child's feelings ("I know you feel sick but since you have no fever you must go to school"). Your child may not be happy with this response but will feel understood and heard. The shaping process begins by giving maximal attention to your child's coping efforts and minimal attention for continued complaints of physical feelings (see chapter 3).

SETTING REALISTIC GOALS

Your first goal is to establish a reasonably peaceful morning routine and help your child get to school on time. Realistically, he may not eat breakfast right away nor be willing to take the school bus. In Jack's case, Susan and Jim didn't initially expect him to eat anything for breakfast. Once his morning routine became more regular, he ate small amounts of French toast. When Jack was willing to try new foods for breakfast and/or lunch, Jim allowed him to listen to music on the way to school.

Homestretch

If your child willingly goes to school, initially allow visits to the nurse as needed. Of course, despite the thermometer's normal readings, some children may still be convinced that they are physically sick. Over time, the frequency of visits to the nurse can be decreased. Ultimately, you want your child to understand that his physical feelings are anxiety related rather than due to real sickness. As your child continues to attend school without actually getting sick, he will learn that his physical feelings are indeed anxiety related.

Unlike Peter, Jack's fear of sickness was simply his body's way of telling him that he was uncomfortable with the process of getting ready for school in the morning. Once he managed this transition, his fear diminished. As a result, Jack did not have any major safety needs nor was it necessary to expose him to any situations other than eating his breakfast in the morning.

Encourage your child to practice relaxation and/or cognitive coping skills (chapter 5). To help your child eat breakfast and/or take the school bus, be sure to follow Peter's and Mark's step-by-step plans (chapter 7).

DYLAN: ENTERING THE SCHOOL BUILDING

Dylan is nine years old, worries about everything, and is very sensitive. He also gets overwhelmed easily, especially in new situations. Getting ready for school is not a problem. Getting out of Roberta's car in the parking lot, however, is another story. Dylan cries, panics, and holds onto his seat for dear life. Roberta simply wants Dylan to enter the school building like other children, without experiencing intense panic.

In order to accomplish this, Dylan needs to take very gradual steps, starting from the parking lot and working his way toward entering the school building. Therefore, Roberta will stay in the car with Dylan in the parking lot, then walk with him toward the school building, and finally help him enter the building with her, alone, and with another safe person.

Next, we'll guide you to structure the beginning exposures for your child who is afraid to enter the school building. If your child's school refusal is expressed differently, please continue to read through this section, since we will be explaining how to structure a gradual set of exposures. You will find specific exposures that are more applicable to your child as we continue to go through each of our real-life examples during this chapter. Let's get started.

Beginning Exposures

The goal is to help your child feel more secure being on the grounds of the school parking lot. For your first exposure, your child should stay in the car with you. Be sure your child understands that he is not expected to enter the school building. Try this a few times, perhaps over the course of a day or two. As your child settles down, ask him to try stepping out of the car and/or offer to walk with him to the school building. If he becomes visibly upset, remain in the parking lot. Expect to remain in the parking lot for as long as one hour. Keep track of how long you remained in the lot and/or how long your child stayed in the car. Consider any of the following to help your child get through the exposure:

- Reassure your child that he can remain in the parking lot but keep encouraging him to take more challenging steps.
- Shape your child's behavior (minimal attention for crying/panic; maximal attention for thinking about and/or taking more challenging steps).
- Remain calm (do your best not to show your frustration/disappointment).
- Help your child practice the cognitive and/or relaxation exercises.
- Use rewards (like trading cards, stickers) to help your child take more challenging steps.

Some children may take several days before they get out of the car. Others may do everything but enter the school building on the first attempt. Be patient. As long as you help your child to feel reasonably secure, his progress will accelerate once he starts walking toward the school building. Of course, if your child misses more than a day or two of school, you may need to enlist the support of school personnel to assist you during this transition. A collaborative working relationship with school personnel will help foster the cooperation needed to implement our program.

Your next step is to change the duration of your child's exposure, then the distance you are from him. For example, when you feel your child is ready, have him step out of the car after five or ten minutes. He will likely only do so if you stay on his side and reassure him that he does not have to walk toward the school building. Once your child feels fairly comfortable being outside of the car, encourage him to wait on the other side of the car from you.

Naturally, this situation will be the most difficult for two reasons. First, your child has to get out of the car. The implication, of course, is that he's now getting ready to walk toward and/or enter the school building. Second, if he remains on his side, he is further away from you.

Your goal is to help your child get out of the car. Although it's ideal for your child to stay on his side, if he cannot do this, do your best to keep the physical contact to a minimum. Encourage your child to take more challenging steps, such as walking toward the school building. Help him practice the coping strategies and consider using some readily available rewards to push him along.

Midway

Now it's time to help your child walk toward the school building. For your first exposure, stay close by and reassure him that there is no expectation of entering the school building.

For some children, this step may need to be repeated several times. Make your praise contingent on your child's willingness to move forward rather than the actual number of steps that he takes. To help your child feel more secure, have him walk toward the school building after all the other students have entered the building. Some children and adolescents also have social fears/anxiety and may worry about being embarrassed or humiliated. We recommend that you continue this sequence of exposures until your child can comfortably remain just outside the school entrance door.

Next, you're ready to help your child enter the school building. In order to minimize the chances that your child will experience intense panic, we recommend that you both walk in, then immediately both walk out. You may need to try this a few times before your child is successful. Once accomplished, your next exposure is to have him walk into the building alone and then immediately walk out while you remain just outside the door.

SETTING REALISTIC GOALS

For both of these situations, we recommend that you have your child enter the school building after all other students have entered. If your child still has difficulty entering the school under these circumstances, consider trying again later in the morning and/or during the early afternoon. Just like getting ready or going to school, entering the school building in the morning may be an overwhelming transition for some children. The good news, however, is that if your child's school refusal is limited to a fear of entering the building, once he gets his foot in the door, the rest of the exposures should go smoothly.

Homestretch

At this point, your child will have demonstrated an ability to spend a brief amount of time in the school building without experiencing panic. Now, it's time for your child to walk to class first with you, then school personnel. If needed as a first step, you can tag along or remain in the hallway until your child gets settled.

In our experience, if your child's school refusal is limited to a fear of entering the school building, you will not have to stay in the hallway very long (perhaps a few minutes). He simply needs some warm-up time to get settled.

Once your child is able to walk to class, you can gradually transfer his key safe person from you to someone who is already present in the school environment, such as his teacher, the school social worker, or his best friend.

If your child has a hard time, you can help him feel more secure by entering the school building with him, as long as he walks to the classroom with the teacher, social worker, or friend.

Eventually, you can move toward remaining in the parking lot. To further challenge your child, consider encouraging him to periodically take the school bus and/or car pool with friends.

Up next is our step-by-step plan to help your child or adolescent manage his fear of staying in school. We illustrate with our real-life stories of Becky and Dan.

BECKY: STAYING IN PRESCHOOL

Becky is four years old and willingly enters her preschool classroom, but only stays if she can sit in the lap of her mother, Rachel. She also refuses to participate in classroom activities or play with the other children. Rachel wants Becky to feel more secure and learn to adapt to the preschool experience without Rachel having to stay for the entire time.

In order to accomplish this, Becky needs to feel comfortable on the school grounds, with the other children, and in the classroom. Therefore, Rachel will first expose Becky to these situations while she remains present and then gradually remove herself, first from the classroom, and then from the school grounds. If your child's school refusal is expressed differently, please continue to read through this section since we will be explaining how to structure a gradual set of exposures for a young child. Let's get started.

Beginning Exposures

Your goal is to help your child become acclimated to the preschool experience. If you anticipate that your child will likely have trouble separating, we recommend exposing him to the school environment either the summer before (if possible) or at least one week prior to the beginning of the school year.

For your first series of exposures, have your child spend some time in his classroom when it's empty, meet with his teacher, and play with a friend on the school grounds. You can consider these exposures as warm-up exercises to help ensure his relatively smooth transition to preschool or kindergarten. Since you will be present for the entire time, he is likely to experience minimal or no school refusal.

If your child still refuses to leave your side and insists that you stay for the entire school day, consider a few more warm-up exposures to help your child feel comfortable at school. First, arrange for your child to have a playdate with a child from school at your house, then work toward having your child play at his friend's house while you stay for the entire time.

Keep the playdates short (one hour) and supervise carefully to ensure that your child has a successful experience. By doing so, you will help your child make the connection that being with friends both during and after school can be fun.

In addition, as an intermediate step, encourage your child to do the following during the school day:

- Leave your side and walk freely around the classroom (you stay nearby).
- Interact with teacher and at least one other child.

Midway

Now it's time to help your child participate in school-related activities with the teacher and his peers. Your goal is to help your child gradually separate from you, and in doing so, become an active participant in the classroom. For your first exposure, have your child join circle time or a similar organized activity with the other children. Reassure your child that he doesn't have to speak or raise his hand, and if needed, he can sit in your lap. Your next step is to change the distance you are from him, such as standing nearby.

If your child is fearful of staying in preschool or kindergarten without you, this situation represents his first major challenge.

He will feel anxious simply because the separation process is beginning. If your child refuses to let you go, you may have to continue sitting on the floor (no physical contact) and gradually move two or three feet away until you can stand out of the way. Also, let your child know that you will stay in the classroom, but only if he makes an effort to participate. Consider using any of the following to help your child get through the exposure:

- Reassure your child ("I'm here . . . I'm not going anywhere").
- Use positive nonverbal body language (smile, wink, thumbs up).

To help your child feel more secure, use your judgment as to how far away you can be from him in the classroom. To get things started, you may have to help your child participate in his activities. As he becomes more comfortable and is distracted by the tasks at hand, move around the classroom as much as you can. Be sure to spend some time hanging around the exit door without being too apparent. When your child can work or play for several minutes without being vigilant of your whereabouts, he is ready for the next step.

Homestretch

This is what you've been waiting for. At this point, your child should be fairly comfortable being at school, participating in classroom activities, and interacting with his peers. Now it's time for your child to learn how to cope without you being present. As a first step, stand by the door as your child works or plays with another child.

When your child notices that you are staying close to the exit door, he may become more anxious and insist on staying with you. Simply reassure him that you are indeed staying in the classroom and help him get back on task. If he seems more vigilant of your whereabouts, once again use positive nonverbal body language to reassure him.

The next step, of course, is for you to temporarily step out of the classroom while your child remains there. You can accomplish this goal by going to the bathroom or retrieving an item from your car in the parking lot. Make sure that your child knows that you're leaving the classroom. The only way he will overcome his school refusal is by confronting and feeling his fear. Consider any of the following to help him get through the exposures:

- Reassure your child that you will be right back.
- Let your child hold your car keys until you return.
- Help your child use relaxation exercises.
- Use rewards (stickers, trading cards, play things).
- Have teacher use distractors (like playing a game).

SETTING REALISTIC GOALS

Some children may have minimal difficulty managing this step. Of course, other children, no matter what is done, will have a great deal of difficulty getting through it.

If your child is like Becky and extremely strong willed, you may need an additional step to help him separate. First, we recommend that you help your child separate outside of school as well. In Becky's case, Rachel and David started leaving Becky with a babysitter (see chapter 7). By doing so, she gradually became more accustomed to letting both parents leave her. Second and more importantly, you may need to change the drop-off pattern in the morning.

For example, Rachel's parenting style (see chapter 3) most closely resembled the protector. As a result, Becky picked up on her mixed signals ("I have to go, but I'm afraid to leave you"). Consequently, David decided to take Becky to school for a few days. Since David's parenting style was similar to the evaluator, Becky did not want to upset him. As a result, Becky not only let her dad go to the bathroom, but she also let him sit in the car for ten minutes. Becky then knew that she could let a parent leave her in the classroom.

If your child gives you a hard time with these situations, consider removing yourself from the school grounds in a more gradual fashion.

Up next is our step-by-step plan to help your adolescent manage his fear of entering and/or staying in school. We illustrate with our real-life story of Dan and his parents, Maggie and Kent.

DAN: GETTING TO THE SCHOOL GROUNDS

Dan is sixteen years old. He gets ready for school but then freezes when it's time to leave. He constantly worries about making mistakes and is terrified of being embarrassed. As a result, he refuses to attend school. Maggie wants Dan to feel more secure about attending school and to realize that his social fears are without merit.

In order to accomplish this, Dan needs to be exposed to the school grounds, his peers, and his classrooms. Let's get started.

Beginning Exposures

The goal is to help your adolescent get to the school grounds. For your first exposure, have him stay in the car with you in the parking lot. If necessary, reassure him that there is no expectation that he enter the school building. Try this a few times until your adolescent begins to feel more secure simply hanging out on the school grounds.

Unlike Dylan, who needed to remain close to his mother to feel safe, Dan does not want to be seen with Maggie. Hanging out in the parking lot gives Dan a chance to scout his best opportunity to enter the school building without being noticed.

If your adolescent gives you a hard time about going to school in the morning, you may need to consider an additional step. For example, Dan refused to leave the house the first two days. Maggie then suggested that she park the car in an out-of-the-way place in the school parking lot. Dan relented, but only after Maggie agreed to park several blocks away from the school. Once all the students entered, Dan was willing to move to the school parking lot. He was then expected to start out from the school parking lot on subsequent school days.

The next step is to have your adolescent walk in the building and then walk out. This step is likely to be very anxiety provoking. Your adolescent may become overwhelmed with social anxiety just thinking about the possibility that someone may approach him. If he gives you a hard time about entering the school building, consider any of the following to help him get through the exposure:

- Encourage practice of the cognitive and/or relaxation exercises.

- Arrive at school during homeroom.

Once your adolescent manages this step, his progress will accelerate as long as you sustain his sense of security.

Midway

Now it's time to have your adolescent spend some time in the school building. First, you can change the duration of your adolescent's exposure, then his access to safe persons. For example, as a first step, your adolescent can spend five minutes in the library. As long as he remains out of sight from his peers, he will likely stay in the library for longer periods of time. A safe person, such as the school guidance counselor or social worker, can also help your adolescent remain in school for thirty minutes.

Up until now, all of the situations involved your adolescent spending brief intervals at school with minimal likelihood of being noticed and/or questioned. A more demanding exposure such as attending homeroom, however, may trigger your adolescent's worst fears of being embarrassed or humiliated.

To increase the likelihood that Dan would be able to complete the exposure, Maggie agreed to remain in the parking lot for the duration of homeroom. In addition, she encouraged Dan to try to stay in school longer (attend first period). If Dan made any effort to stay in school, he was allowed to call his father, Kent, on his cell phone.

Dan was unable to leave the parking lot on his first two attempts to attend homeroom. He panicked over the possibility of a social confrontation. If your adolescent gives you a hard time about attending homeroom, be sure to help prepare him for an inevitable social confrontation. We illustrate with the following dialogue (see chapter 5) between Dan and his mother, Maggie.

Dan: I can't go to homeroom.

Maggie: Why not?

Dan: What would I say?

Maggie: You've spent time in school. Anyone approach you?

Dan: Shakes head.

Maggie: Anyone give you strange looks?

Dan: No . . . but they could be talking about me.

Maggie: Have you heard that anyone is talking about you?

Dan: No.

Maggie: What is likely to happen if you attend homeroom?

Dan: Someone might ask questions about why I've been gone so much.

Maggie: Do you usually talk to people during homeroom?

Dan: Not really.

Maggie: Any friends in homeroom?

Dan: Some.

Maggie: Would they bother you?

Dan: No . . .

Maggie: So what are the chances of someone bothering you?

Dan: Pretty slim.

Maggie: Doesn't sound like anyone will bother you; but if they do, what can you say?

Dan: I don't know.

Maggie: How about strep throat or a viral infection?

Dan: I guess so.

Maggie: What's the best thing that could happen?

Dan: I'll be left alone.

Maggie: Anything else?

Dan: Can't think of anything.

Maggie: Maybe your friends will be happy to see you . . .

Dan: Maybe.

Maggie: Will you try to attend homeroom?

Dan: Okay . . .

To help build Dan's confidence, Maggie and Kent encouraged social exposures outside of the school setting. For example, Dan was also avoiding other social situations such as going to the mall, movies, or a restaurant. What if he was noticed or recognized? How would he explain why he's not in school? As long as Dan agreed to go to some of these places, Maggie and Kent allowed him to choose their location.

Naturally, Dan opted to go out of town to minimize his chances of being recognized. Nevertheless, he still worried about the possibility of a social confrontation. Surprisingly, he did see an acquaintance who was actually pleased to catch up with him. As a result of these exposures, not only did Dan attend homeroom, he also stayed for two periods.

SETTING REALISTIC GOALS

Once adolescents start attending academic classes, their continued progress will vary. For instance, some individuals may immediately stay for the entire school day. Others, however, may continue to have sporadic attendance.

For example, in Dan's case, he quickly progressed to staying for the morning classes through lunch. He also had several days in which he remained at school for the entire day. However, on test days or scheduled athletic events, he often complained of feeling sick and tried to stay home from school. Performance anxiety is often a key component of social anxiety–related school refusal.

For this reason, it's important to set realistic goals for your adolescent. The idea is to help him attend school for a minimum amount of time (say, two classes, or half a day) *consistently*, regardless of how he feels. As your adolescent becomes more comfortable in the school setting, you can gradually increase the minimal attendance requirement until a full day is reached. You may have to adjust your expectations on days when performance issues emerge (like tests, athletic events, concerts).

Naturally, parenting styles play a role here. For example, once Dan attended school for the full day, Maggie (evaluator) insisted that he do so every day. Kent (protector), on the other hand, was more willing to allow Dan to stay home if Dan felt sick or appeared nervous about performance-oriented events.

If you find yourself in this kind of situation, work together with your spouse or partner to determine a mutually acceptable minimal attendance requirement. In addition, be sure to discuss appropriate rewards for your adolescent's efforts that exceed the minimal attendance requirement.

WORKING WITH SCHOOLS

As you know, helping your adolescent attend and/or stay in school is no easy task. Imagine, just as you begin to feel hopeful that a normal school routine is inevitable, your adolescent shuts down and refuses to leave the house.

Ideally, you will be working together with personnel from your adolescent's school to develop a plan for his gradual return. However, if teacher(s) and/or school personnel don't fully understand the level of your adolescent's anxiety, they may end up overemphasizing the timely completion of missed assignments, rather than continuing to help him feel secure. Your adolescent may respond to this perceived pressure by shutting down.

Of course it's important for both you and the school to hold your adolescent responsible for his work. But, if he cannot resume full-time attendance, other educational arrangements (like temporary home instruction) may need to be considered. For this reason, it's important to work with school personnel to develop a plan that initially emphasizes your adolescent's gradual return to school but also allows for the flexible completion of his work.

Homestretch

This is what you've been waiting for. At this point, your adolescent will have demonstrated an ability to regularly stay in school for a specified amount of time. Now it's time for him to work toward full-time attendance while you gradually eliminate family involvement.

To increase the likelihood of Dan being able to fully attend school during test days and/or athletic events, Maggie and Kent helped arrange (with the school) for Dan to initially observe rather than to participate if he felt unprepared. In most cases, however, Dan chose to participate and performed satisfactorily. Simply knowing that he *could* observe was all that he needed to help him feel secure. Dan was also allowed extra time when taking tests and provided with a flexible schedule to complete any missed assignments. These concessions helped Dan progress to full-time attendance within two weeks. Dan, however, was still calling his dad as many as five times per day.

Clearly, it was necessary to limit Dan's access to his father during the school day. As a first step, Maggie and Kent allowed Dan a maximum of two phone calls per day. In addition, these phone calls were for touching base and could last a maximum of two minutes each. Given Kent's very supportive and overprotective nature, however, he was unable to limit the amount of time per call (usually over ten minutes each).

For this reason, Dan was then only allowed to call Maggie a maximum of two times. Given her firmer and more critical nature, calling her was not as appealing as calling his dad. As a result, Dan called at most two times per week.

At this point, Dan was no longer allowed to call either parent. If circumstances required getting in touch with his parents (for instance, an actual illness), school personal assumed responsibility for doing so. Dan, however, was still allowed an ongoing pass to meet with his guidance counselor for five minutes a maximum of two times per day. Once again, simply knowing that he could meet with his guidance counselor helped Dan feel more secure. Dan continued full-time attendance, and, at most, met with his guidance counselor two times per week.

Summary

In this chapter, we helped you manage your child or adolescent's fear of going and/or staying in school. In chapter 10, we'll help you evaluate your child or adolescent's overall progress and determine whether seeking professional help would be beneficial.

Chapter 10

Taking the Next Step

I thought Lenore was over this [sighs]. *We found her in our bed this morning.*

—Kate

CHAPTER OBJECTIVES

In this chapter you will learn:

- How to make sense of your child's progress
- Some benefits of working with a mental health professional

WHERE ARE WE NOW?

If you followed our lessons and step-by-step plans, your journey was likely a demanding one and, hopefully, rewarding. Let's take a moment to rate your child's overall progress. Please the circle the number that best reflects her improvement following the program.

1 Refused to try

2 Very resistant (no change)

3 Some effort shown (small changes)

4 Some items achieved (from fears list)

5 Most items achieved (from fears list)

6 All items achieved (from fears list)

In our experience, most parents rate their child's progress in the four to six range. Many children successfully negotiate all of the situations from their separation-fears list. Of course, some children are very resistant to confronting their fears and may only achieve marginal or no recognizable signs of improvement.

In the next section, we help you understand the reasons behind your child's overall level of progress so that you can take steps to foster her continued improvement.

MAKING SENSE OF YOUR CHILD'S PROGRESS

When evaluating your child's progress it's important to take into account factors that are specific to your child's separation anxiety, her personality, and any additional problems that she is experiencing.

Your Child's Separation Anxiety

Factors specific to your child's separation anxiety may include:

- Type of separation anxiety
- Length of separation-anxious concerns
- How much it interferes with functioning

Of the four types of separation anxiety, a fear of being alone due to the possibility of getting sick (the follower) is the easiest to help your child negotiate. This is especially true if your child is young, like Debbie, and is primarily afraid of being alone during the day.

As your child's separation fears creep into the nighttime, management may become increasingly complicated. Being alone is naturally more challenging as things go bump in the night. The darkness, unknown noises, and belief in supernatural figures may give credence to the development of intruder fears.

When it comes to helping your child manage her fear of sleeping alone, it's best to act quickly. The longer your child has avoided sleeping alone, the more resistant she will become when encouraged to do so. If your child has been sleeping in your bedroom for more than six months, professional help may be necessary to complete the program.

Customarily, however, separation fears tend to cause the most disruption as they extend beyond a child's home environment. For example, Peter and Mark's abandonment fears also interfered with their academic and social functioning.

Regardless of the nature of your child's separation anxiety, her personality will be a big factor in determining her overall success.

Your Child's Personality

Factors specific to your child's personality may include her:

- Temperamental style
- Motivation to overcome separation anxiety

If your child is strong willed like Debbie and Mark, helping her will be a greater challenge regardless of the type and seriousness of her separation anxiety. She may continually resist your efforts to expose her to separation-related situations. As a result, your child may negotiate fewer items from her separation-fears list.

On one hand, it's understandable if you feel disappointed in your child's progress and view her behavior as oppositional. But remember, resistance is an important and expected part of the process. For some children, breaking down the wall of anxiety takes longer than for others. You may be close, and if so, progress is right around the corner. Because of your efforts, the hard part may be almost over.

Your child's resistance may also be related to her willingness to overcome separation anxiety. For example, your child may not understand why you're asking her to give up her security and/or may not want to, no matter how sizable the reward. This is often the case if your child's separation anxiety has persisted for some time and/or you are her key safe person.

For example, if your child is like Lenore, Mark, or Becky, she may have a difficult time trusting someone other than you to keep her safe. Children, like Debbie and Peter, with varied safe persons and objects are often more willing to confront their separation fears. Of course, it's also possible that your child's resistance may have little to do with her personality or degree of motivation. The culprit may be additional problems that your child is experiencing.

Your Child's Additional Problems

Children with separation anxiety often experience additional problems such as:

- School refusal
- Worry, panic, OCD, shyness/social anxiety
- Sadness, depression, social withdrawal
- Learning challenges, low frustration tolerance, ADD/ADHD

In our real-life examples, the children and adolescents' problems were largely limited to separation fears and/or mild-to-moderate school refusal resulting from panic or social anxiety. The presence of any *severe* additional problems will lessen a child's already shaky sense of security. What may look like strong resistance (refusing to try) may be a child's way of showing that she is completely overwhelmed. The more debilitating the anxiety problem becomes (through avoidance), the greater likelihood that social withdrawal and depression will emerge.

For example, both chronic (sporadic school attendance for a year or greater) and severe (a month or more of consecutive absences) school refusal rarely respond effectively to a parent-assisted coping-skills program as described in this book. In such cases, serious depression, social phobia, or panic attacks are usually involved.

Under these circumstances, more comprehensive therapist-assisted programs and/or medication that addresses both anxiety and related problems are often necessary. We'll discuss this issue in more detail later in the chapter.

Trauma and Separation Anxiety

Up until now we've been discussing separation anxiety and school refusal that's largely based on a child or adolescent's irrational fears (having minimal or no evidence of occurring). Sometimes, however, separation anxiety (as well as other problems) may result from serious threats of injury or actual harm to a child and/or close family members. For example, trauma-related separation anxiety may develop from personal experience involving any of the following:

- Severe car accident
- Being the victim of a burglary
- Being the victim of physical, emotional, or sexual abuse (including bullying)
- Being kidnapped
- Being the victim of a manmade or natural disaster
- Being the victim of a terrorist attack (or having a family member who was a victim)
- Unexpected death of a family member or close relative

It's not surprising that six months after the events surrounding the September eleventh terrorist attack that almost 30 percent of New York City public school children were identified as having probable anxiety or depressive disorders. In their large-scale survey of 8,236 children from fourth through twelfth grade, researchers at Columbia University Medical Center found that agoraphobia (14.8 percent), separation anxiety (12.3 percent), and post-traumatic stress (10.6 percent) were the most prevalent disorders. Anxiety-related symptoms associated with trauma may include:

- Physical symptoms (stomachaches, headaches)
- Frightening nightmares
- Generalized anxiety
- Clinginess
- Fears of being alone and/or sleeping alone
- School refusal

Given the similarity of anxiety symptoms, trauma may sometimes be mistaken for separation fears that are irrational or stemming from insecure parent-child attachments. How can you tell the difference?

First, determine whether your child or a close family member actually experienced a traumatic event (like a burglary or unexpected injury/death). In most cases, like our real-life stories, there is insufficient evidence to suggest that trauma played a role. Sometimes, however, the trauma may remain unknown, especially if a child is fearful of potential repercussions regarding its revelation (for instance, in sexual abuse).

What's even more important than the actual event is an individual's reaction to the event. For example, two people are involved in a car accident that could have resulted in serious injury or death. Remarkably, both individuals escape relatively unharmed physically. However, one person returns to work the next day while the other remains incapacitated for some time. For events to be considered traumatic, one must respond with intense fear and horror.

A third factor to consider is the extent of your child's adjustment difficulties. For example, like our real-life stories, fear-based separation anxiety is often limited to situations involving being alone and/or abandoned. When separation anxiety results from trauma, however, it interferes more significantly with the child's level of daily functioning. In addition to anxiety-related symptoms, trauma may elicit any of the following in a child or adolescent:

- Confusion
- Agitation
- Flashbacks (reexperiencing the event)
- Difficulty remembering events associated with the trauma
- Less interest in participating in pleasant activities (not just separation related)
- Difficulty concentrating
- Depression and/or social withdrawal
- Sensitive startle response

If you suspect that your child's separation anxiety is more than fear based, do not hesitate to seek professional help to have her properly evaluated.

THE BENEFITS OF PROFESSIONAL HELP

Let's face it. When it comes to helping our own children, being objective is no easy task. We're too close to the situation.

Sometimes, the guidance of an unbiased third party can make all the difference in helping children overcome separation anxiety and/or school refusal. Professional guidance can assist you with issues of accountability, goal setting, and backsliding.

Accountability

Was helping your child overcome her separation anxiety one big power struggle? Strong-willed children often view any kind of limit setting as intrusive. If asking your child to clean her room provokes an angry reaction, it's not surprising that she vehemently resists separation-related confrontations. Too many power struggles can leave any parent feeling overwhelmed and exhausted. This is especially true if social supports are lacking (for example, a single parent or uninvolved spouse or partner).

A qualified therapist will set effective limits with your child. You will no longer be perceived as bad or mean since the therapist now becomes responsible for assigning the anxiety-provoking exposures. As your child progresses through her separation-fears list, the therapist will help you set effective limits on your own and support you in doing so.

Goal Setting

Every child is unique and progresses at her own pace. Some children make rapid progress in a matter of weeks. Others take their time and proceed in a more cautious manner. Goal setting may also be influenced by one's parenting style.

For example, the evaluator may push her child too hard. The peacekeeper may not push at all. The protector may continue to give in to her child's separation anxiety. Setting realistic goals becomes even more challenging when parents or partners have differing styles. A qualified therapist can help you structure your child's program to maximize her success. This is especially true if your child is experiencing any additional problems.

Backsliding

At this point, you're probably wondering when the program ends. How long does your child have to keep practicing the coping strategies? When can you finally forget about your child's separation anxiety?

As we mentioned before, your child's avoidance of separation-anxiety situations can indeed be minimized or eliminated. Depending upon the circumstances, you may be successful doing this on your own or may need some assistance from a mental health professional. What still remains, however, is your child's sensitivity to anxiety. This means that periodically she may backslide.

It is expected that your child will occasionally show signs of separation anxiety, even after successfully conquering her fears. If your child slips, there is no need to panic. You're not back to square one. Slipping often results when a child stops practicing the coping strategies, experiences stress, or anticipates separation-related transitions (like the beginning of school or camp). Lenore occasionally ends up in her parent's bedroom if she has a nightmare and Mark still gives his mother a hard time about new (unfamiliar) situations.

To minimize slips, we encourage you to continue to challenge your child. Exposures need not be separation related. Any time your child confronts a difficult situation, she will experience anxiety. Continued exposures will help build your child's confidence and prepare her to cope effectively with future situations.

Another benefit of working with a qualified therapist is that they will incorporate periodic follow-ups into the program. These visits can be used as refreshers if your child's coping skills become rusty or as problem solvers in anticipation of stressful transitions.

GETTING YOUR LIFE BACK

In the beginning of the book we discussed the importance of getting your life back. As a loving parent, you are entitled to certain basic privileges and should not have to give them up at the expense of helping your child overcome separation anxiety and/or school refusal. These privileges include:

- Sleep
- Hope for a peaceful morning routine
- Hobbies, exercise, or other recreational activities
- Social life
- Free time
- Freedom
- Privacy

Customarily, most parents that complete our program have worked hard to help their child overcome separation anxiety and/or school refusal. As a result, some serenity is restored to the morning and/or nighttime routines. During the process, however, the same investment is not always made to enhance a parent's social well-being. This may be due to a number of reasons.

For example, in some cases, the time commitment required to help a child overcome separation anxiety precludes any efforts for parents to cultivate a social life. More typically, however, some parents of separation-anxious youth do not feel comfortable engaging in regular social/recreational activities during their childrearing years. They feel that family should be of central importance. And while we agree that family should be a priority, we've found that effective parenting often results when parents also take care of their own needs. This is especially true when a child or adolescent has anxiety and/or behavioral issues. Respite and pleasant activities for caregivers are important components of a healthy family process. If you've been reluctant or simply haven't had time to pursue your own interests, take small steps (like your child's exposures) toward a more active lifestyle. Both you and your family will benefit.

TAKING CARE OF YOUR OWN MENTAL HEALTH

Nurturing one's own needs and/or seeking professional help for a child are important steps but may not always result in effective solutions. Sometimes, however, parents may also need professional help to take care of their own mental health needs.

For example, any parent can easily become overwhelmed from the stress of dealing with a child's separation anxiety and/or school refusal. Being able to handle such problems without experiencing undue stress may not be realistic, especially if a child's anxiety is severe and/or additional problems need to be addressed.

Under these circumstances, parents may become vulnerable to experiencing their own anxiety, depression, or physical problems. Chronic fatigue, worry, and/or social withdrawal may then limit parents' ability to help their child. Stress resulting from other sources such as family conflict, marital issues, or a lack of emotional/financial support (for instance, in a divorce, for a single parent, or if the parent is unemployed) can also interfere with parents' ability to help their child.

Sometimes parents' ability to help a child is not hampered by ongoing family stress, but rather their own sensitivity to anxiety. As you know, anxiety runs in families. Parents of anxious youth are more likely to experience anxiety themselves. An overly anxious parenting style (the protector) may encourage fearful behaviors through modeling and discourage exposures through avoidance. Such a parenting style only becomes problematic when a parent is unable to follow through with the most basic exposures.

In such cases, because of a parent's own anxiety, any distress that a child experiences may be too painful for the parent to endure.

In our own work with anxious youth and their families, we regularly recommend therapy for parents as a first step or in conjunction with a child's treatment program. As you can see, depending upon your family's circumstances, there are many ways to address your child's anxiety and/or behavioral issues. Taking advantage of the different options will not only help your child overcome separation anxiety and related problems, but also facilitate a healthier family environment. In the next section, we examine some of these treatment options.

TREATMENT OPTIONS

In this section, we briefly discuss cognitive behavioral therapy, family-based treatment, and medication. Let's begin with cognitive behavioral therapy since this treatment is most consistent with the approach described in this book.

Cognitive Behavioral Therapy

Cognitive behavioral therapy (CBT) is an action-oriented therapy that emphasizes both the teaching and application of specific skills for targeted behavioral problems. CBT is typically short-term (usually three to six months of weekly sessions), focuses largely on the child or adolescent's current problems, and may include any of the following components:

- Child and/or parent anxiety management education
- Parent training
- Relaxation exercises
- Problem-solving strategies

- Cognitive therapy techniques
- Real-life exposures
- Relapse prevention

The parenting program described in this book is evidence-based and draws on many years of clinical research. In general, treatment outcome research shows that 50 percent to 80 percent of anxious youth benefit from CBT-oriented programs. The success rate for separation-anxious youth has been shown to be as high as 96 percent (Eisen and Schaefer 2005).

In choosing a qualified CBT-trained therapist, be sure that the individual appears knowledgeable regarding anxiety management strategies. Most importantly, ask questions about the role of real-life exposures in their treatment program. As you know, effective and regular exposures will be critical to your child or adolescent's success in overcoming separation anxiety and related problems. Finally, find out the extent to which the therapist works with parents during the treatment program. CBT programs that include parent participation are more likely to result in long-term treatment successes. This finding is supported by our own work with separation-anxious youth as well as years of clinical research.

Although most CBT-trained therapists tend to be licensed clinical psychologists, other professionals, such as psychiatrists, social workers, and licensed counselors may have received some training as well. Be sure to ask about the therapist's specific training and background. To assist you in finding an anxiety specialist in your area, please refer to our helpful resources list at the end of the book.

Family-Based Treatment

Family therapists view childhood problems as stemming from the family unit as a whole. For example, rather than focusing specifically on a child's separation anxiety, a family therapist may examine both the interactions and communication patterns of all the members of a given family. Thus, the goal of treatment is to change the problematic family interaction.

Family therapists also emphasize structural changes within a family. This means that change occurring in one person will promote changes in other family members as well. For example, what happens to untreated siblings when another child receives more attention for separation anxiety or school refusal? The untreated siblings may soon experience separation-anxious behaviors as well to get equal attention. A family therapist closely monitors these kinds of situations.

Family therapists also view the family unit as ever changing and sensitive to life events. For example, what happens to the family unit as the oldest child leaves home? The younger siblings may develop separation anxiety as their parents respond with increased overprotectiveness.

Family-based treatment approaches to help anxious youth have not received the overwhelmingly positive research results that CBT has. For this reason, we recommend CBT as a first step. In our experience, family therapy can be especially helpful for children and adolescents who experience severe anxiety and/or many additional problems. For example, chronic school refusal can be quite complicated, often involves problematic family interactions, and rarely responds to one specific treatment. In these situations, a combination of therapies (CBT and family therapy) as well as medication is often needed.

Medications

In our experience, most children with separation anxiety respond favorably to therapy and will not be candidates for medication. On rare occasions, however, medication may be needed for a child with intruder fears, especially if she hasn't slept for weeks.

Customarily, medication is considered for the additional problems (like ADHD, depression, trauma) that a child or adolescent experiences, or when anxiety is chronic and/or severe (in the form of OCD, panic attacks, social phobia, or school refusal). Even in these situations, in light of safety concerns and side effects, considering medication for a child can be a daunting dilemma.

As psychologists, we believe in the power of CBT and other evidence-based psychological treatments. But at the same time, we also understand that many childhood problems are influenced by biological sensitivities to emotional experiences. For this reason, medication clearly has value and at times may be instrumental in helping a child or adolescent begin the process of overcoming anxiety and related problems.

For example, sometimes children or adolescents shut down when experiencing severe or chronic anxiety. If this occurs, psychological treatments may be of minimal benefit. Medication in these instances may help to reduce the crisis so psychological treatments can be utilized. It's best to think of medication as one potential option to consider among many. The treatment of choice for severe anxiety problems is often the combination of CBT and medication.

If your child or adolescent's circumstances require considering medication, we recommend working with a child/adolescent psychiatrist that specializes in anxiety and related problems. Such an individual can carefully monitor whether your child improves with medication as well as any potential side effects experienced. Your child's pediatrician is likely to be a valuable resource in helping you find a qualified professional. Our list of helpful resources can also assist you in this process.

Summary

Whether you followed the lessons of our program on your own or worked with a qualified professional, you've taken important steps to enhance your child's ability to confront and conquer her separation anxiety. By doing so, she will move toward a more comfortable and secure way of life.

Resources

We imagine that some of your questions still remain unanswered or that you may be thinking about seeking professional help. In this section, you will find relevant organizations and renowned university-based child anxiety clinics that can be of assistance as well as a source for appropriate referrals.

ORGANIZATIONS

Anxiety Disorders Association of America
8730 Georgia Avenue, Suite 600
Silver Spring, MD 20910
240-485-1001
www.adaa.org

The Anxiety Panic Internet Resource
www.algy.com/anxiety

The Association for Behavioral and Cognitive Therapies
305 7th Avenue, 16th Floor
New York, NY 10001-6008
212-647-1890
www.aabt.org or www.abct.org

The Child Anxiety Network
www.childanxiety.net

National Association of School Psychologists
www.nasponline.org

National Institute of Mental Health
www.nimh.nih.gov

CHILD ANXIETY CLINICS

Boston University
Center for Anxiety and Related Disorders
Child and Adolescent Fear and Anxiety Treatment Program
648 Beacon Street, 6th Floor
Boston, MA 02215
617-353-9610
www.bu.edu/anxiety

University of California, Los Angeles
Childhood OCD and Anxiety Program
300 UCLA Medical Plaza, Suite 1315
Los Angeles, CA 90095
310-825-4132
www.npi.ucla.edu/caap

Duke University
Child and Adolescent Anxiety Disorders Program
Child and Family Study Center
718 Rutherford Street
Durham, NC 27705
919-416-2447
www2.mc.duke.edu/pcaad

Fairleigh Dickinson University
Child Anxiety Disorders Clinic
Center for Psychological Services
131 Temple Avenue
Hackensack, NJ 07601
201-692-2593
www.fdu.edu/centers/cps/cadc.html
http://alpha.fdu.edu/ucoll/ps/anxiety.html

Florida International University
Child Anxiety and Phobia Program
University Park Campus
Deuxieme Maison Building, 2nd Floor
Miami, FL 33199
305-348-1937
www.fiu.edu/~capp

University of Hawaii
Child and Adolescent Stress and Anxiety Program
Center for Cognitive Behavior Therapy
2430 Campus Road
Honolulu, HI 96822
808-956-9559
www2.hawaii.edu/~chorpita/casap.html

University of Illinois at Chicago
Pediatric Stress and Anxiety Disorders Clinic
1747 W. Roosevelt Road, Room 155
Chicago, IL 60608
312-355-0194
www.psych.uic.edu/clinical/PSADC

University of Maryland
Maryland Center for Anxiety Disorders
2109 Biology Psychology Building
College Park, MD 20742
301-405-0232
www.anxietydisorderscenter.org

University of Nevada, Las Vegas
School Refusal and Anxiety Disorders Clinic
4505 Maryland Parkway
Las Vegas, NV 89154
702-895-0184

New York University
Child Study Center
Institute for Anxiety and Mood Disorders
557 First Avenue
New York, NY 10016
212-263-6622
www.aboutourkids.org

Ohio State University
Anxiety and Stress Disorders Clinic
223 Townshend Hall
1885 Neil Avenue
Columbus, OH 43210
614-292-2345
http://anxiety.psy.ohio-state.edu

Temple University
Child and Adolescent Anxiety Disorders Clinic
Weiss Hall
13th Street and Cecil B. Moore Avenue
Philadelphia, PA 19122
215-204-7165
www.childanxiety.org

Virginia Tech University
Child Study Center
460 Turner Street
Collegiate Square, Suite 207
Blacksburg, VA 24061
540-231-8276
www.childstudycenter.vt.edu

FURTHER READING

Barlow, D. H. 2004. *Anxiety and its Disorders*. New York: Guilford Press.

Eisen, A. R., and C. E. Schaefer. 2005. *Separation Anxiety in Children and Adolescents: An Individualized Approach to Assessment and Treatment*. New York: Guilford Press.

Kearney, C. A. 2001. *School Refusal in Youth. A Functional Approach to Assessment and Treatment*. Washington, DC: American Psychological Association.

Kendall, P. C. 1992. *Coping Cat Workbook*. Ardmore, PA: Workbook Publishing.

Kendall, P. C. 2005. *Child and Adolescent Therapy: Cognitive-Behavioral Procedures*. 3rd Edition. New York: Guilford Press.

Kendall, P. C., E. Flannery-Schroeder, S. Panichelli-Mindell, M. Southam-Gerow, A. Henin, and M. Warman. 1997.

Therapy for youth with anxiety disorders: A second randomized clinical trial. *Journal of Consulting and Clinical Psychology* 65:366-380.

LaGreca, A. M., W. K. Silverman, E. M. Vernberg, and M. C. Roberts. 2002. *Helping Children Cope with Disasters and Terrorism*. Washington, DC: American Psychological Association.

Morris, T. L., and J. S. March. 2004. *Anxiety Disorders in Children and Adolescents*. New York: Guilford Press.

Ollendick, T. H., and J. S. March. 2004. *Phobic and Anxiety Disorders in Children and Adolescents*. New York: Oxford University Press.

Rapee, R., et al. 2000. *Helping Your Anxious Child: A Parent's Step-By-Step Guide*. Oakland, CA: New Harbinger Publications.

References

Barlow, D. H. 2002. *Anxiety and Its Disorders: The Nature and Treatment of Anxiety and Panic.* 2nd ed. New York: Guilford Press.

Beck, J. S. 1995. *Cognitive Therapy: Basics and Beyond*. New York: Guilford Press.

Bogels, S., and D. Zigterman. 2000. Dysfunctional cognitions in children with social phobia, separation anxiety disorder, and generalized anxiety disorder. *Journal of Abnormal Child Psychology* 28:205-211.

Drabman, R. S., and D. L. Creedon. 1979. Beat the buzzer. *Child Behavior Therapy* 1:295-296.

Eisen, A. R., and C. E. Schaefer. 2005. *Separation Anxiety in Children and Adolescents: An Individualized Approach to Assessment and Treatment*. New York: Guilford Press.

Lonigan, C. J., M. W. Vasey, B. M. Philips, and R. A. Hazen. 2004. Temperament, anxiety, and the processing of threat-relevant stimuli. *Journal of Clinical Child and Adolescent Psychology* 33:8-20.

Ollendick, T. H. 1998. Panic disorder in children and adolescents: New developments, new directions. *Journal of Clinical Child Psychology* 27:234-245.

Ollendick, T. H., and J. A. Cerny. 1981. *Clinical Behavior Therapy with Children*. New York: Kluwer/Plenum Press.

Rapee, R. M. 1997. Potential role of childrearing practices in the development of anxiety and depression. *Clinical Psychology Review* 17:47-67.

Andrew R. Eisen, Ph.D., is an associate professor in the School of Psychology and director of the Child Anxiety Disorders Clinic at Fairleigh Dickinson University. His research and clinical interests include child anxiety and related problems, learning disorders, and sensory integration issues. Eisen has published numerous articles and chapters and four books including **Separation Anxiety in Children and Adolescents**. He maintains private practices focusing on children and families in Bergen County, NJ and in Rockland County, NY.

Linda B. Engler, Ph.D., is codirector of the Child Anxiety and Related Disorders Clinic in Rockland County, NY. Her research and clinical interests include child anxiety and related problems, ADHD, and the early detection and remediation of nonverbal and language-based learning disorders. Engler has published and presented in the areas of anxiety disorders, ADHD, eating disorders, and school partnerships. In addition, she maintains a private practice focusing on children and families in Rockland County, NY.

Foreword writer **Joshua D. Sparrow, MD,** is coauthor of the Brazelton Way books.

Some Other New Harbinger Titles

The Courage to Trust, Item 3805 $14.95
The Gift of ADHD, Item 3899 $14.95
The Power of Two Workbook, Item 3341 $19.95
Adult Children of Divorce, Item 3368 $14.95
Fifty Great Tips, Tricks, and Techniques to Connect with Your Teen, Item 3597 $10.95
Helping Your Child with OCD, Item 3325 $19.95
Helping Your Depressed Child, Item 3228 $14.95
The Couples's Guide to Love and Money, Item 3112 $18.95
50 Wonderful Ways to be a Single-Parent Family, Item 3082 $12.95
Caring for Your Grieving Child, Item 3066 $14.95
Helping Your Child Overcome an Eating Disorder, Item 3104 $16.95
Helping Your Angry Child, Item 3120 $17.95
The Stepparent's Survival Guide, Item 3058 $17.95
Drugs and Your Kid, Item 3015 $15.95
The Daughter-In-Law's Survival Guide, Item 2817 $12.95
Whose Life Is It Anyway?, Item 2892 $14.95
It Happened to Me, Item 2795 $17.95
Act it Out, Item 2906 $19.95
Parenting Your Older Adopted Child, Item 2841 $16.95
Boy Talk, Item 271X $14.95
Talking to Alzheimer's, Item 2701 $12.95
Helping a Child with Nonverbal Learning Disorder or Asperger's Syndrome, Item 2779 $14.95
The 50 Best Ways to Simplify Your Life, Item 2558 $11.95

Call **toll free, 1-800-748-6273,** or log on to our online bookstore at **www.newharbinger.com** to order. Have your Visa or Mastercard number ready. Or send a check for the titles you want to New Harbinger Publications, Inc., 5674 Shattuck Ave., Oakland, CA 94609. Include $4.50 for the first book and 75¢ for each additional book, to cover shipping and handling. (California residents please include appropriate sales tax.) Allow two to five weeks for delivery.

Prices subject to change without notice.

